CONTENTS

Beginner

Easy

Intermediate   Experienced

EARFLAP Hat

YOU'LL NEED:

YARN
3½oz/100g or 220yd/200m of any worsted weight variegated wool yarn

NEEDLES
One size 7 (4.5mm) circular needle, 16"/40cm long
or size to obtain gauge
One set (5) size 7 (4.5mm) double-pointed needles (dpns)

ADDITIONAL MATERIALS
One size H/8 (5mm) crochet hook
Stitch holder
Stitch marker

KNITTED MEASUREMENTS
Circumference 20"/51cm
Length 10"/25.5cm from lower edge of earflap to top (not including pompom)

GAUGE
18 sts and 28 rows to 4"/10cm over St st using size 7 (4.5mm) needles.
Take time to check gauge.

STITCH GLOSSARY
Pattern Stitch in rows
(over an even number of sts)
Row 1 (RS) *K1, p1; rep from * to end.
Row 2 and all even rows Purl.
Row 3 *P1, k1; rep from * to end.
Row 4 Purl.
Row 5 Knit.
Row 7 Rep row 5.
Row 8 Purl.
Rep rows 1–8 for pat st in rows.
Note For pat stitch in rnds work same as pat stitch in rows only knit all even numbered rnds.

EARFLAP
Cast on 9 sts. Work 4 rows in pat st.
Row 5 (inc RS) Inc 1 st in first st, knit to last 2 sts, Inc 1 st in next st, k1—11 sts.
Row 6 Purl.
Row 7 Rep inc row—13 sts.
Cont in pat st, rep inc row every 2nd row, then every 4th row until there are 25 sts.

Rep inc row every other row twice more—29 sts. Purl one row. Cut yarn. Place sts on holder.
Rep for 2nd earflap.
Next (joining) rnd With circular needle, rejoin yarn, k sts of first earflap inc'ing 9 sts evenly across, cast on 7 sts, k sts of 2nd earflap inc'ing 9 sts evenly across, cast on 7 sts, pm for beg of rnd, join to work in the rnd—90 sts.
Work even in pat as established until piece measures 3"/7.5cm from joining rnd, end with a pat rnd 4.

Shape crown
Note Change to dpns when sts no longer fit comfortably on circular needle.
Next (dec) rnd [K4, SKP, k3, k2tog, k4] 6 times—78 sts. K 1 rnd.
Next (dec) rnd [K3, SKP, k3, k2tog, k3] 6 times—66 sts. K 1 rnd.
Next (dec) rnd [K2, SKP, k3, k2tog, k2] 6 times—54 sts. K 1 rnd.
Work rnds 1–4 of pat st.
Next (dec) rnd [K1, SKP, k3, k2tog, k1] 6 times—42 sts. K 1 rnd.
Next (dec) rnd [SKP, k3, k2tog] 6 times—30 sts. K 1 rnd.
Work rnds 1–4 of pat st.
Next (dec) rnd *K1, k2tog; rep from * around—20 sts. K 1 rnd.
Next (dec) rnd *K2, k2tog; rep from * to last st, k1. Thread yarn twice through rem 14 sts. Fasten off.

FINISHING
Trim
With crochet hook and RS facing, beg at corner of one earflap and work 1 rnd of hdc around edge of hat,

working 2 hdc into each earflap corner. Join with sl st at end of rnd. Fasten off.
Ties (make 2)
Make chain 10"/25.5cm long.
Work 1 hdc into front lp of each ch st. Work 2 hdc into last ch. Work 1 hdc into back lp of each ch st. Join with sl st and fasten off.
Pompoms
Make two 2"/5cm pompoms and attach to ends of ties. Attach ties to lower edge of earflaps.
Make one 3"/7.5cm pompom and attach to top of hat.

Paul Amato for lvarepresents.com

COLORFUL Earflap Hat

Eye[4]Media

KNITTED MEASUREMENTS
Circumference 20"/51cm
Length (excluding earflap) 10"/25.5cm

GAUGE
21 sts and 24 rows/rnds to 4"/10cm over St st using size 7 (4.5mm) needles.
Take time to check gauge.

NOTE
When changing colors foll chart, bring new yarn from underneath working yarn to avoid holes in work.

CAP
Beg at lower edge with dpns and MC, cast on 100 sts. Divide sts evenly on 4 needles with 25 sts on each needle. Join, being careful not to twist sts on needles and pm to mark beg of rnd. P2 rnds.
Next rnd With F, knit, inc 2 sts on each of the 4 dpn—108 sts total and 27 sts on each dpn.
Beg chart 1
Rnd 1 Beg with rnd 1 of chart 1, work 12-st rep 9 times around. Cont to foll chart 1 through rnd 36.
Shape top
Beg chart 2
Rnd 1 With MC, knit.
Rnd 2 With MC, work as foll:
Needle 1 Ssk, k to last 2 sts, k2tog;
Needle 2 Ssk, k to last 2 sts, k2tog;
Needle 3 Ssk, k to last 2 sts, k2tog;
Needle 4 ssk, k to last 2 sts, k2tog—100 sts.
Rnds 3 and 5 Rep rnd 1.
Rnds 4 and 6 Rep rnd 2—84 sts.
Rnds 7 and 8 Foll chart 2, work even with A and B.
Rnds 9, 11 and 13 Rep rnd 1.
Rnds 10, 12 and 14 Rep rnd 2—60 sts.
Rnds 15 and 16 Foll chart 2, work even with C and F.
Rnds 17, 19 and 21 Rep rnd 1.
Rnds 18, 20 and 22 Rep rnd 2—36 sts.
Rnds 23 and 24 Foll chart 2, work even with D and E.
Cont rem of cap with MC only.
Rnds 25, 27 and 29 With MC, knit.
Rnds 26, 28 and 30 Rep rnd 2—12 sts .
Rnds 31, 32 and 33 With MC, knit.
Rnd 34 [SK2P] 4 times—4 sts. Cut yarn leaving an end for sewing top.
Pull through rem 4 sts and draw up tightly to secure. Fasten off.

EAR FLAPS (make 2)
Fold hat in half and mark center 25 sts on one side of cap and center 25 sts on other side of cap.
For first flap, with RS facing and using MC and straight needles, pick up and k 25 sts under the MC rolled edge (that is, pick up sts in the first A row). Working

back and forth in rows, p1 row on WS. Then work 4 rows more in St st dec 1 st on last WS row—24 sts.
Beg chart 3
Row 1 (RS) Foll row 1 of chart 3, work 4-st rep 6 times across.
Row 2 Work even foll chart.
Next (dec) row (RS) Cont to foll chart 3, k1, ssk, k to last 3 sts, k2tog, k1.
Next row Cont to foll chart, purl.
Rep last 2 rows, foll chart 3 through row 18, then cont with MC only until 2 sts rem. Bind off 2 sts on last WS row.
Earflap trim
Working from RS at right edge of one earflap, with B, pick up and k22 sts evenly along this edge only to point. K1 row. Bind off knitwise. Then with C, pick up along left edge from point to top and work in same way. Sew trim tog at point.

FINISHING
Block hat flat. Make a 1½"/4cm pom-pom with E, attach to top of cap.

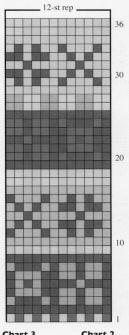

Chart 1
12-st rep

36
30
20
10
1

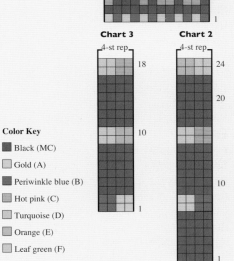

Chart 3
4-st rep

18
10
1

Chart 2
4-st rep

24
20
10
1

Color Key
■ Black (MC)
□ Gold (A)
■ Periwinkle blue (B)
■ Hot pink (C)
□ Turquoise (D)
□ Orange (E)
□ Leaf green (F)

RAPUNZEL Hat

Jack Deutsch

YOU'LL NEED:

YARN 6
Wool Ease Thick and Quick by Lion Brand Yarn Co., 6oz/170g, 106yd/97m, acrylic and wool blend
3 balls in taupe

NEEDLES
One pair size 13 (9mm) needles
or size to obtain gauge

ADDITIONAL MATERIALS
Cable needle (cn)

KNITTED MEASUREMENTS
Circumference 22"/56cm

GAUGE
9 sts and 12 rows to 4"/10cm over St st using size 13 (9mm) needles.
Take time to check gauge.

STITCH GLOSSARY
8-st LC Sl next 4 sts to cn and hold in *front*, k4, k4 from cn.
8-st RC Sl next 4 sts to cn and hold in *back*, k4, k4 from cn.

HAT
Cast on 47 sts.
Next row (RS) K1, *p1, k1; rep from * to end. Rep this row once more, inc 3 sts evenly spaced—50 sts.
Beg cable pat
Row 1 (RS) K18, p1, k12, p1, k18.
Row 2 and all WS rows P18, k1, p12, k1, p18.
Row 3 K18, p1, 8-st LC, k4, p1, k18.
Rows 5 and 7 Rep row 1.
Row 9 K18, p1, k4, 8-st RC, p1, k18.

Row 11 Rep row 1.
Row 12 Rep row 2. Rep rows 1–12 until piece measures 6½"/16.5cm from beg, end with a RS row.
Crown shaping
Row 1 (WS) *P3, p2tog; rep from * to end—40 sts.
Rows 2 and 4 Knit.
Row 3 Purl.
Row 5 *P2, p2tog; rep from * to end—30 sts.
Row 6 Knit.
Row 7 [P2tog] 15 times—15 sts. Cut yarn leaving a 20"/51cm tail and thread through rem sts. Pull tog tightly and secure end, then sew back seam.

BRAIDS
Sections (make 6)
Cast on 5 sts. Work in St st until piece measures 48"/122cm from beg, when slightly stretched. Bind off. Allow edges to curl to center. Sew cast-on edges of 3 sections tog. Braid the 3 sections, then sew the bound-off edges tog to secure braid. Make another braid. Beg at top of hat with cast-on end of braid, pin braid to side of hat, positioning it approx 3"/7.5cm from center cable. Sew side edges of braid in place. Sew rem braid on to opposite side of hat.

TASSELS
Wind yarn 12 times around a 4"/10cm piece of cardboard. Make 2 tassels and attach to bound-off ends of braids.

POMPOM
Make a 4½"/11.5cm diameter pompom and sew to top of hat.

BOBBLE Helmet

Marcus Tullis

YOU'LL NEED:

YARN (4)
3½/100g (5¼oz/150g, 5¼oz/150g) or 330yd/300m (490yd/450m, 490yd/450m) of any worsted weight wool yarn.

NEEDLES
One size 7 (4.5mm) circular needle, 16"/40cm length
or size to obtain gauge
One set (5) size 7 (4.5mm) double-pointed needles (dpns)

ADDITIONAL MATERIALS
One pair size 8 (5mm) needles
Stitch markers

KNITTED MEASUREMENTS
Circumference 18 (21½, 22½)"/45.5 (53.5, 57)cm

GAUGE
15 sts and 30 rows to 4"/10cm over St st using size 7 (4.5mm) needles.
Take time to check gauge.

STITCH GLOSSARY
Make Bobble (MB) Knit 6 sts into the same st, turn, sl 1, purl 5, turn, sl 1, knit 5, turn, [k2tog] 3 times, turn, SK2P.

HAT
With size 7 (4.5mm) circular needle, cast on 66 (78, 84) sts. Place marker for beg of row and join for knitting in the round, taking care not to twist sts.

Brim
Rnds 1, 3, 5 Purl. **Rnds 2, 4, 6, 7** Knit. **Rnds 8 and 14** *MB, k5; rep from * around. **Rnds 9 and 15** *K1 tbl, k5; rep from * around. **Rnd 10** Knit. **Rnd 11** K3, *MB, k5; rep from * to last 2 sts, k2. **Rnd 12** K3, *k1 tbl, k5; rep from * to last 2 sts, k2. **Rnd 13** Knit. Work even in St st until piece measures 6¾ (7, 7½)"/17 (18, 19)cm from beg.

Crown shaping
Shape crown as foll, switching to dpns when sts no longer comfortably fit on circular needles:
Rnd 1 *K4, k2tog; rep from * around—55 (65, 70) sts. **Rnd 2 and all even rnds** Knit. **Rnd 3** *K3, k2tog; rep from * around—44 (52, 56) sts. **Rnd 5** *K2, k2tog; rep from * around—33 (39, 42) sts. **Rnd 7** *K1, k2tog; rep from * around—22 (26, 28) sts. **Rnd 9** *K2tog; rep from * around—11 (13, 14) sts. Cut yarn leaving 6"/15cm tail, thread yarn through rem sts and pull tightly to close.

Right earflap
With size 8 (5mm) needles, RS facing, hat upside down and beg 2"/5cm to left of marker, pick up and knit 15 (17, 19) sts.
Row 1 and all odd rows Purl. **Rows 2 and 4** Sl 1, k to last st, sl 1. **Row 6 (dec row)** Sl 1, ssk, k to last 3 sts, k2tog, sl 1—13 (15, 17) sts. Rep dec row every other row until 5 sts rem. Purl 1 row. **Next row (RS)** K1, SK2P, K1—3 sts. Work I-cord tie as foll: *Knit one row. Without turning work, slip the sts back to other end of needle. Pull yarn tightly from the end of the row. Rep from * for 13"/33cm. Cut yarn with a 6"/15cm tail. Thread through rem sts and cinch to close. Knot I-cord 1"/2.5cm from end.

Left earflap
Fold hat in half at marker. Mark position of earflap on left side of hat, pm and work as for Right Earflap.

RIBBED Beret

Paul Amato for lareepresents.com

YOU'LL NEED:

YARN [3]
5¼oz/150g or 350yd/320m of any DK weight wool yarn.

NEEDLES
Sizes 5 and 6 (3.75 and 4mm), 16"/40cm long
or size to obtain gauge
1 set (5) size 6 (4mm) double-pointed needles (dpns)

ADDITIONAL MATERIALS
Stitch marker
One ¾" (19mm) button (optional)

KNITTED MEASUREMENTS
Circumference 20"/50.5cm
Diameter after blocking 10"/25.5cm

GAUGE
24 sts and 32 rnds to 4"/10cm over k2, p2 rib using larger needles.
Take time to check gauge.

STITCH GLOSSARY
K1, P2 Rib
Rnd 1 *K1, p2; rep from * around.
Rep rnd 1 for k1, p2 rib.
K2, P2 Rib
*K2, p2; repeat from *around.
Rep rnd 1 for k2, p2 rib.

BRIM
With smaller needles, cast on 126 sts loosely. Join, being careful not to twist sts, and pm for beg of rnd. Work in k1 p2 rib until piece measures 1½"/ 4cm from beg.
Next rnd (inc) *K1, p2, M1; rep from * around—168 sts.
Crown
Change to larger needles. Work in k2, p2 rib until piece measures 6½"/16.5cm from beg.
Next rnd [K28, pm] 5 times, k to end.
Shape top
Note Change to dpns when sts no longer fit comfortably on circular needle.
Rnd 1 *Ssk, work in pat as established to 2 sts before next marker, k2tog, sm; rep from * around—12 sts dec'd.
Rnd 2 (and all even rnds) Work even in pat as established.
Rep rnds 1 and 2 for 12 times more—12 sts rem.
Next (dec) rnd *K2tog, repeat from * around—6 sts.

Cut yarn and thread tail through rem sts to close.

FINISHING
Stretch beret over a 10"/25.5cm dinner plate. Steam to block.

Sew button to top if desired.

RUCHED Beret

KNITTED MEASUREMENTS
Brim circumference 20"/51cm
Diameter 9"/23cm

GAUGE
18 sts and 28 rnds to 4"/10cm over St st using size 8 (5mm) needles. *Take time to check gauge.*

BERET
With one dpn, cast on 16 sts for top, leaving long tail.
Set-up row With dpn #1, *K2, place marker (pm), k2; rep from * for dpn's #2, 3, 4. Join, being careful not to twist sts, pm for beg of rnd.
Rnd 1 [P1, yo, p1] 8 times—24 sts.
Begin chart
Note Change to circular needle when stitches no longer fit on dpns.

Beg with rnd 2, work chart repeat 8 times around. Cont to work chart in this manner until rnd 34 is complete—35 sts in each rep, 280 sts total.

BRIM
Next (dec) rnd *K2, k2tog; rep from * around—210 sts.
Purl one rnd.
Next (dec) rnd *K1, k2tog; rep from * around—140 sts.
Purl one rnd.
Next (dec) rnd *K2tog; rep from * around—70 sts.
Purl one rnd.
Next (eyelet) rnd *Yo, k2tog; rep from * around.
Next rnd Purl.
Next rnd Knit.
Bind off.

YOU'LL NEED:

YARN ④
Wool-Ease by Lion Brand Yarn Co., 3oz/85g, 197yd/180m, acrylic and wool blend
1 skein in #196 zinniat

NEEDLES
One size 8 (5mm) circular needle 16"/40cm long *or size to obtain gauge*
One set (5) size 8 double-pointed needles (dpns)

ADDITIONAL MATERIALS
Stitch markers

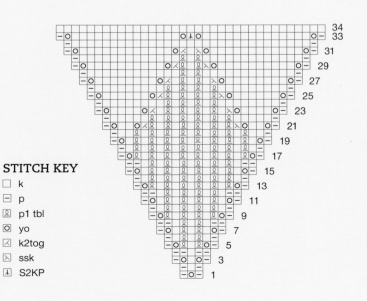

STITCH KEY
☐ k
⊟ p
▣ p1 tbl
⊙ yo
⧄ k2tog
⧅ ssk
⊥ S2KP

WAVY Cabled Hat

YOU'LL NEED:

YARN
3½oz/100g or 270yd/240m of any DK weight wool yarn

NEEDLES
One pair each sizes 3 and 5 (3.25 and 3.75mm) needles
or size to obtain gauge

ADDITIONAL MATERIALS
Cable needle (cn)

KNITTED MEASUREMENTS
Circumference 21"/53cm
Length (excluding earflaps) 8"/20.5cm

GAUGE
28 sts and 30 rows to 4"/10cm over chart pat using size 5 (3.74mm) needles.
Take time to check gauge.

STITCH GLOSSARY
4-ST RPC (This cable st is not used in chart pats) Sl next st to cn and hold to *back*, k3, p1 from cn.
5-ST RPC Sl next 2 sts to cn and hold to *back*, k3, p2 from cn.
5-ST LPC Sl next 3 sts to cn and hold to *front*, p2, k3 from cn.
6-ST RC Sl next 3 sts to cn and hold to *back*, k3, k3 from cn.
6-ST LC Sl next 3 sts to cn and hold to *front*, k3, k3 from cn.

CAP
First earflap
With size 5 (3.75mm) needles, cast on 15 sts. Beg earflap chart as foll:
Row 1 (RS) Inc 1 st in first st, p1; 5-st LPC, [k1, p1] 3 times, inc 1 st in next st, k1—17 sts.
Row 2 Inc 1 st in first st, [p1, k1] 4 times, p3, k3, inc 1 st in next st, k1—19 sts.
Row 3 Inc 1 st in first st, p5, k3, [k1, p1] 3 times, k2, inc 1 st in next st, k1—21 sts.
Row 4 P4, [k1, p1] 4 times, p2, k6, p1.

Row 5 Inc 1 st in first st, p6, k4, [p1, k1] 3 times, k2, inc 1 st in next st, k1—23 sts.
Row 6 P5, [k1, p1] 4 times, p2, k6, p2.
Row 7 Inc 1 st in first st, k1, p4, 5-st RPC, [k1, p1] 3 times, k4, inc 1 st in next st, k1—25 sts.
Row 8 P6, [k1, p1] 5 times, p2, k4, p3.
Row 9 Inc 1 st in first st, k2, p2, 5-st RPC, [k1, p1] 3 times, k1, 5-st RPC, k1, inc 1 st in next st, k1—27 sts.
Row 10 K1, p3, k2, p3, [k1, p1] 5 times, p2, k2, p3, k1.
Row 11 Inc 1 st in first st, k3, 5-st RPC, [k1, p1] 3 times, k1, 5-st RPC, p2, k2, inc 1 st in next st, p1—29 sts.
Row 12 P1, k1, p3, k4, p3, [k1, p1] 5 times, p5, k1, p1.
Row 13 Inc 1 st in first st, k1, 6-st RC, [k1, p1] 3 times, k1, 5-st RPC, p4, k3, inc 1 st in next st, k1—31 sts.
Cont to foll earflap chart in this way on 31 sts through row 32. Cut yarn. Leave these sts on a holder.

Second Earflap
Work as for first earflap. Do not cut yarn.
Next row (RS) At beg of row cast on 11 sts, then [p1, k1] 3 times, 5-st RPC, * k6, p2, 5-st RPC, [k1, p1] 3 times, k1, 5-st RPC, k6 *, turn. Cast on 69 sts, then working across the 31 sts of first earflap from holder, rep between *'s, turn. Cast on 10 sts—152 sts.

Beg panel pat
Foundation row (WS) K1, working from left to right, work row 24 of panel pat chart, working 25-st rep a total of 6 times, k1. Beg and end with k1, work rows 1–24 of panel pat as established until piece measures approx 6"/15cm from beg of cap above earflaps, ending with row 20 of panel pat chart.

Eye[4]Media

Shape top
Note Cont to work a k1 selvage st at each end of row (not included in the instructions below) and work as foll:
Row 1 (RS) [K1, p3tog, k1, p1, k1, 6-st LC, k3, p4, 5-st RPC] 6 times.
Row 2 [P1, k1, p3, k4, p9, (k1, p1) twice, k1] 6 times.
Row 3 [P3tog, 5-st RPC, k6, p2, 5-st RPC, k1, p1] 6 times—128 sts.
Row 4 *[P1, k1] twice, p3, k2, p6, k2, p3, k1; rep from * 5 times more.
Row 5 Work 4-ST RPC, *p2, k6, 5-st RPC, p3tog, 5-st RPC; rep from * to last 17 sts, p2, k6, 5-st RPC, p3tog, p1—116 sts.
Row 6 [P1, k1] twice, *p9, k4, p3, k3; rep from * to last 15 sts, p9, k3, p3.
Row 7 K3, p3tog, *k3, 6-st RC, p3, k3, p1, p3tog; rep from * to last 13 sts, k3, 6-st RC, p3tog, p1—102 sts.
Row 8 K2, *p9, k2, p3, k3; rep from * to last 13 sts, p9, k1, p3.
Row 9 K3, p1, *k9, p3tog, k3, p2; rep from *

to last 11 sts, k9, p2tog—91 sts.

Row 10 K1, *p9, k2, p3, k1; rep from * to last 13 sts, end p9, k1, p3.

Row 11 K3, k2tog, k8, *p1, 5-st LPC, k9; rep from * to last st, p1—90 sts.

Row 12 K1, *p12, k3; rep from * to last 12 sts, p12.

Row 13 *[Sl next 3 sts to cn and hold to back, k3, then k2tog, k1 from cn] twice, p3; rep from *, end p1—78 sts.

Row 14 K1, *p10, k3; rep from * to last 10 sts, p10.

Row 15 *K10, p3tog; rep from * to last 11 sts, k10, p1—68 sts.

Row 16 *K1, p10; rep from * to end.

Row 17 *K10, p1; rep from * to end.

Row 18 Rep row 16.

Row 19 *[Sl next 3 sts to cn and hold to back, k2, k3tog from cn] twice, p1; rep from * to end—44 sts.

Row 20 *K1, p6; rep from * to end.

Row 21 *K2tog, k2, SKP, p1; rep from * to end—32 sts.

Row 22 *K1, p4; rep from * to end.

Row 23 *K3tog tbl, SKP; rep from * to end—14 sts. Beg with a purl row, work 7 rows in St st. Cut yarn leaving a long end for sewing seam, and draw through rem 14 sts, draw up tightly and secure.

FINISHING
Block flat to measurements.
Lower edging
With smaller needles and RS facing, pick up and k sts around lower edge as foll: 9 sts along left back edge, 23 sts along one side of earflap, 15 sts along cast-on edge of earflap, 23 sts along other side of earflap, 60 sts along front cast-on edge, 23 sts along side of earflap, 15 sts along cast-on edge of earflap, 23 sts along other side of earflap, 9 sts along right back edge—200 sts. K2 rows. Bind off knitwise.

Twisted cord (make 2)
Cut 6 strands of yarn, 23"/59cm long. Make a twisted cord and attach to each earflap. Sew back seam.

Stitch Key

☐	K on RS, p on WS
⊟	P on RS, k on WS
	5-ST LPC
	5-ST RPC
	6-ST LC
	6-ST RC

PANEL PAT CHART

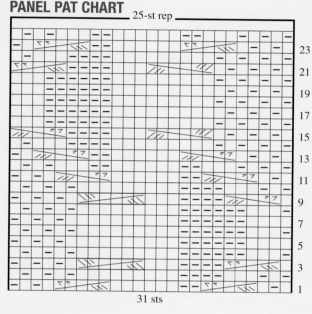

25-st rep

31 sts

23 21 19 17 15 13 11 9 7 5 3 1

EARFLAP CHART

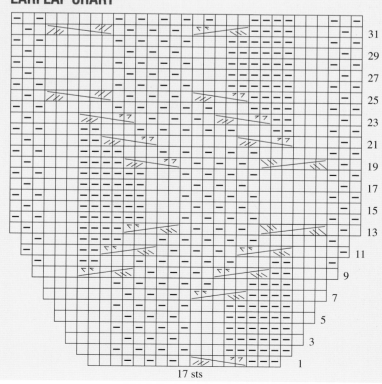

17 sts

31 29 27 25 23 21 19 17 15 13 11 9 7 5 3 1

BASKETWEAVE Hat

YOU'LL NEED:

YARN (3)
3½oz/100g or 230yd/210m of any DK
weight wool yarn

NEEDLES
Size 5 (3.75mm) circular needle,
16"/40cm long
or size to obtain gauge
One set (5) size 5 (3.75mm)
double-pointed needles (dpns)

ADDITIONAL MATERIALS
Stitch marker

KNITTED MEASUREMENTS
Circumference 20"/51cm
Length 7"/18cm

GAUGE
24 sts and 36 rnds to 4"/10cm over
basketweave pat using size 5 (3.75mm)
needles.
Take time to check gauge.

STITCH GLOSSARY
Basketweave Pattern (multiple of 8 sts)
Rnds 1–4 *K4, p4, rep from * around.
Rnds 5–8 *P4, k4, rep from * around.
Rep rnds 1–8 for basketweave pat.

HAT
Cast on 120 sts and join, being careful
not to twist sts. Place marker for beg of
rnd. Work in basketweave pat until hat
measures 4"/10cm from beg, end with a
rnd 4 or 8.
Beg crown
P 2 rnds. K 1 rnd.
Next (rib) rnd [K14, p6] 6 times around.

Rep rib rnd 6 times more.
Shape crown
Next (dec) rnd [Ssk, k10, k2tog, p6] 6 times
around—108 sts.
Next 5 rnds [K12, p6] 6 times around.
Next (dec) rnd [Ssk, k8, k2tog, p6] 6 times
around—96 sts.
Next 4 rnds [K10, p6] 6 times around.
Next (dec) rnd [Ssk, k6, k2tog, ssp, p2,
p2tog] 6 times around—72 sts.
Next 3 rnds [K8, p4] 6 times around.
Next (dec) rnd [Ssk, k4, k2tog, p4] 6 times
around—60 sts.
Next 2 rnds [K6, p4] 6 times around.
Next (dec) rnd [Ssk, k2, k2tog, ssp, p2tog] 6

times around—36 sts.
Next rnd [K4, p2] 6 times around.
Next (dec) rnd [Ssk, k2tog, p2tog] 6 times
around—18 sts.
Next (dec) rnd [K2tog, p1] 6 times
around—12 sts.
Next (dec) rnd [K2tog] 6 times around—6 sts.
Break yarn and thread through rem sts.

10

POMPOM Flair

Paul Amato for livarepresents.com

YOU'LL NEED:

YARN 5
3½ oz/100g or 220yd/200m of any bulky weight wool yarn

NEEDLES
One size 10 (6mm) circular needle, 16"/40cm long
or size to obtain gauge

ADDITIONAL MATERIALS
Stitch marker

KNITTED MEASUREMENTS
Circumference 17½"/44.5cm
Length 8½"/21.5cm

GAUGE
18 sts and 24 rows to 4"/10cm over pat st using size 10 (6mm) needles.
Take time to check gauge.

STITCH GLOSSARY
Broken Rib
Rnds 1–3 *K2, p1; rep from * around.
Rnd 4 Purl.
Rep rnds 1–4 for broken rib.

BEANIE
With circular needle, cast on 78 sts. Join, being careful not to twist sts, place marker for beg of rnd.
Rnds 1 and 2 *K2, p1; rep from * around.
Rnd 3 Purl.
Beg broken rib pat.
Work in broken rib pat until piece measures 6"/15cm from beg, end with a rnd 4.
Shape crown
Next rnd *K2, p1; rep from * around.
Next (dec) rnd *K2tog, p1; rep from * around—52 sts.

Next rnd *K1, p1; rep from * around
Next rnd Purl.
Next rnd Knit.
Next (dec) rnd *K2tog, k1; rep from *, end k1—35 sts.
Next rnd Knit.
Next rnd Purl.
Next (dec) rnd *K1, k2tog; rep from * to last 2 sts, k2tog—23 sts.
Next rnd Knit.
Next (dec) rnd *K1, k2 tog; rep from * to last 2 sts, k2tog—15 sts.
Next rnd Knit.
Next (dec) rnd [K2tog] 7 times, k1—8 sts.
Next rnd Knit.
Cut yarn leaving 12"/30.5cm tail.
Thread yarn through rem sts. Fasten off.

FINISHING
Make 5"/12.5cm pompom. Sew pompom to top of hat.

POMPOM Panache

YOU'LL NEED:

YARN ④
5½oz/160g or 220yd/200m of any worsted weight wool blend yarn

NEEDLES
One pair each size 8 and 9 (5 and 5.5mm) needles
or size to obtain gauge

ADDITIONAL MATERIALS
Cable needle (cn)

KNITTED MEASUREMENTS
Circumference 19½"/49.5cm

GAUGE
17 sts and 21 rows to 4"/10cm over St st using larger needles.
Take time to check gauge.

STITCH GLOSSARY
2-st RT Knit 2nd st on LH needle, then k first st; sl both sts off LH needle.
3-st LPC Sl next 2 sts to cn and hold in *front*, p1, k2 from cn.
3-st RPC Sl next st to cn and hold in *back*, k2, p1 from cn.
3-st LC Sl next 2 sts to cn and hold in *front*, k1, k2 from cn.
3-st RC Sl next st to cn and hold in *back*, k2, k1 from cn.
4-st LC Sl next 2 sts to cn and hold in *front*, k2, k2 from cn.

6-st LC Sl next 3 sts to cn and hold in *front*, k3, k3 from cn.

Cable Rib (multiple of 4 sts)
Row 1 (RS) P2, *2-st RT, p2; rep from * to end.
Row 2 K2, *p2, k2; rep from * to end.
Rep rows 1 and 2 for cable rib.

Cable Panel A (over 4 sts)
Row 1 (RS) K4.
Row 2 P4.
Row 3 4-st LC.
Row 4 P4.
Rep rows 1—4 for cable panel A.

Cable Panel B (over 22 sts)
Row 1 (RS) P4, 3-st RC, p1, 6-st LC, p1, 3-st LC, p4.
Row 2 K4, p2, k1, p8, k1, p2, k4.
Row 3 P3, 3-st RPC, k1, p1, k6, p1, k1, 3-st LPC, p3.
Row 4 K3, p3, k1, p8, k1, p3, k3.
Row 5 P2, 3-st RC, p1, k1, p1, k6, p1, k1, p1, 3-st LC, p2.
Row 6 K2, p2, k1, p1, k1, p8, k1, p1, k1, p2, k2.
Row 7 P1, 3-st RPC, [k1, p1] twice, 6-st LC, [p1, k1] twice, 3-st LPC, p1.
Row 8 K1, p3, k1, p1, k1, p8, k1, p1, k1, p3, k1.
Row 9 P1, 3-st LPC, [k1, p1] twice, k6, [p1, k1] twice, 3-st RPC, p1.
Row 10 Rep row 6.
Row 11 P2, 3-st LPC, p1, k1, p1, k6, p1, k1, p1, 3-st RPC, p2.
Row 12 Rep row 4.
Row 13 P3, 3-st LPC, k1, p1, 6-st LC, p1, k1, 3-st RPC, p3.
Row 14 Rep row 2.
Row 15 P4, 3-st LPC, p1, k6, p1, 3-st RPC, p4.
Row 16 K5, p12, k5.
Rep rows 1–16 for cable panel B, AT THE SAME TIME, work 6-st LC over center 6 sts every 6 rows.

CAP
Cuff
With smaller needles, cast on 94 sts. Work in cable rib for 3½"/9cm, end on a WS row.
Next (inc) row P across inc 12 sts evenly

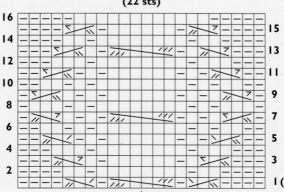

Cable Panel B (22 sts)

16 | | 15
14 | | 13
12 | | 11
10 | | 9
8 | | 7
6 | | 5
4 | | 3
2 | | 1 (RS)

Cable Panel A (4 sts)

4 | 3
2 | 1 (RS)

STITCH KEY

☐ K on RS, P on WS

⊟ P on RS, K on WS

(WS) ☐☐ Seed St (RS)

⊠ 2-st RT

3-st RC

3-st LC

3-st RPC

3-st LPC

4-st LC

6-st LC
(worked over center 6 sts every 6 rows)

spaced—106 sts. Change to larger needles.

Note WS of ribbed cuff is RS of crown.

Crown

Row 1 (RS) P2, *2-st RT, p2, work row 1 of cable panel A across next 4 sts, p2*; rep from * to * 3 times more, 2-st RT, work row 1 of cable panel B across next 22 sts; rep from * to * 4 times.

Row 2 *K2, work row 2 of cable panel A across next 4 sts, k2, p2*; rep from * to * 3 times more, work row 2 of cable panel B across next 22 sts, p2; rep from * to * 4 times, k2. Cont to work in pat sts as established until piece measures 7"/18cm from beg, end with a WS row.

Crown shaping

Dec row 1 (RS) P2, *2-st RT, p2tog, work cable panel A across next 4 sts, p2tog*; rep from * to * 3 times more, 2-st RT, work cable panel B across next 22 sts; rep from * to * 4 times—90 sts. Cont to work in pat sts as established for 11 rows.

Dec row 2 (RS) P2, *2-st RT, p1, ssk, k2tog, p1*; rep from * to * 3 times more, 2-st RT, work cable panel B across next 22 sts; rep * to * 4 times—74 sts.

Next row K1, [p2, k1] 7 times, p2, work cable panel B across next 22 sts, [p2, k1] 8 times, p2, k2.

Dec row 3 (RS) P2, [2-st RT, p1] 8 times, 2-st RT, work cable panel B across next 22 sts, [2-st RT, p1] 8 times. Cont to work cable panel B as established, rep last 2 rows once more.

Next row [K1, p2] 8 times, work cable panel B across next 22 sts, [p2, k1] 8 times, p2, k2.

Dec row 4 (RS) P2tog, [k2tog, p1] 8 times, k2tog, work cable panel B across next 22 sts, [k2tog, p1] 8 times—56 sts.

Next row [K1, p1] 8 times, work cable panel B across next 22 sts, [p1, k1] 9 times.

Dec row 5 (RS) *K2tog; rep from * to end—28 sts. Cut yarn leaving a 20"/51cm tail and thread through rem sts. Pull tog tightly and secure end, then sew back seam, rev seam over last 3"/7.5cm for cuff turnback.

Pompom Make a 4"/10cm diameter pompom and sew to top of cap.

YOU'LL NEED:

YARN
3½oz/100g or 220yd/210m of any worsted weight variegated wool yarn

NEEDLES
Size 7 (4.5mm) circular needle, 16"/40cm long *or size to obtain gauge*
One set (4) size 7 (4.5mm) double-pointed needles (dpns)

ADDITIONAL MATERIALS
Cable needle (cn)
Stitch marker

KNITTED MEASUREMENTS
Circumference 19½"/49.5cm

GAUGE
22 sts and 27 rnds to 4"/10cm over cable pat using size 7 (4.5mm) circular needle. *Take time to check gauge.*

STITCH GLOSSARY
4-st LC Sl next 2 sts to cn and hold in *front*, k2, k2 from cn.

CABLE PATTERN
(multiple of 12 sts)
Rnds 1 and 2 (RS) *P2, k4; rep from * around.
Rnd 3 *P2, 4-st LC, p2, k4; rep from * around.
Rnds 4 and 5 Rep rnd 1.
Rep rnds 1–5 for cable pat.

HAT
With circular needle, cast on 108 sts. Join taking care not to twist sts on needle. Place marker for end of rnd and sl marker every rnd. Work in cable pat, rep rnds 1–5 for 7 times.

Crown shaping
Note Change to dpns (dividing sts evenly between three needles) when there are too few sts on circular needle.

Rnd 1 *P2, k4, p2, k2, k2tog; rep from * around—99 sts.
Rnd 2 *P2, k4, p2, k3; rep from * around.
Rnd 3 *P2, 4-st LC, p2, k1, k2tog; rep from * around—90 sts.
Rnd 4 *P2, k4, p2, k2; rep from * around.
Rnd 5 *P2, k4, p2, k2tog; rep from * around—81 sts.
Rnd 6 *P2, k4, p2, k1; rep from * around.
Rnd 7 *P2, k4, p1, k2tog; rep from * around—72 sts.
Rnd 8 *P2, 4-st LC, p1, k1; rep from * around.
Rnd 9 *P2, k4, k2tog; rep from * around—63 sts.
Rnd 10 *P2, k5; rep from * around.
Rnd 11 *P2, k3, k2tog; rep from * around—54 sts.
Rnd 12 *P2, k2, k2tog; rep from * around—45 sts.
Rnd 13 *P2, k1, k2tog; rep from * around—36 sts.
Rnd 14 *P2, k2tog; rep from * around—27 sts.
Rnd 15 *P1, k2tog; rep from * around—18 sts.
Rnd 16 [K2tog] 9 times—9 sts. Cut yarn leaving a 8"/20.5cm tail and thread through rem sts. Pull tog tightly and secure end.

Jack Deutsch

LACE Slouch

KNITTED MEASUREMENTS
Circumference 22"/56cm
Length 10"/25.5cm

GAUGES
21 sts and 32 rows to 4"/10cm over St st using larger needles.
21 sts and 32 rnds to 4"/10cm over lace pat using larger needles.
Take time to check gauge.

BRIM
With smaller needles, cast on 112 sts, divided evenly on 4 dpns. Join, being careful not to twist sts, and pm for beg of rnd.

around. Rep this rnd for k1, p1 rib until piece measures 2"/5cm from beg. Change to larger needles.

Beg lace pat
Rnd 1 (inc) *Yo, k2tog, yo, p12, yo, k2tog, yo, k12, rep from * around—120 sts.
Rnd 2 K3, *p12, k18, rep from * around, end last rep k15.
Rnd 3 (inc) *Yo, k2tog, yo, k13, rep from * around—128 sts.
Rnd 4 Knit.
Rnd 5 (inc) *Yo, k2tog, yo, p14, yo, k2tog, yo, k14, rep from * around—136 sts.
Rnd 6 K3, *p14, k20, rep from * around, end last rep k17.
Rnd 7 (inc) *Yo, k2tog, yo, k15, rep from * around—144 sts.
Rnd 8 Knit.

YOU'LL NEED:
YARN 3
3½oz/100g or 280yd/250m of any DK weight wool yarn.
NEEDLES
One set (5) each size 6 and 7 (4 and 4.5mm) double-pointed needles (dpns)
or size to obtain gauge
ADDITIONAL MATERIALS
Stitch marker

Rnd 9 (inc) *Yo, k2tog, yo, p16, yo, k2tog, yo, k16, rep from * around—152 sts.
Rnd 10 K3, *p16, k22, rep from * around, end last rep k19.
Rnd 11 (inc) *Yo, k2tog, yo, k17, rep from * around—160 sts.
Rnd 12 Knit.
Rnd 13 (inc) *Yo, k2tog, yo, p18, yo, k2tog, yo, k18, rep from * around—168 sts.
Rnd 14 K3, *p18, k24, rep from * around, end last rep k21.
Rnd 15 (inc) *Yo, k2tog, yo, k19, rep from * around—176 sts.
Rnd 16 Knit.
Rnd 17 *Yo, k2tog, yo, p18, p2tog, yo, k2tog, yo, k18, k2tog, rep from * around.
Rnd 18 K3,* p19, k25, rep from * around, end last rep k22.
Rnd 19 *Yo, k2tog, yo, k18, k2tog, rep from * around.
Rnd 20 Knit.
Rnds 21–32 Rep rnds 17–20 three times more.

Shape Crown
Rnd 1 (dec) *Yo, k2tog, yo, p2tog tbl, p16, p2tog, yo, k2tog, yo, ssk, k16, k2tog, rep from * around—168 sts.
Rnd 2 K3, *p18, k24, rep from * around, end last rep k21.
Rnd 3 (dec) *Yo, k2tog, yo, ssk, k15, k2tog, rep from * around—160 sts.
Rnd 4 Knit.
Rnd 5 (dec) *Yo, k2tog, yo, p2tog tbl, p14, p2tog, yo, k2tog, yo, ssk, k14, k2tog, rep from * around—152 sts.
Rnd 6 K3, *p16, k22, rep from * around, end last rep k19.
Rnd 7 (dec) *Yo, k2tog, yo, ssk, k13, k2tog, rep from * around—144 sts.
Rnd 8 Knit.
Rnd 9 (dec) *Yo, k2tog, yo, p2tog tbl, p12, p2tog, yo, k2tog, yo, ssk, k12, k2tog, rep

from * around—136 sts.
Rnd 10 K3, *p14, k20, rep from * around, end last rep k17.
Rnd 11 (dec) *Yo, k2tog, yo, ssk, k11, k2tog, rep from * around—128 sts.
Rnd 12 Knit.
Rnd 13 (dec) *Yo, k2tog, yo, p2tog tbl, p10, p2tog, yo, k2tog, yo, ssk, k10, k2tog, rep from * around—120 sts.
Rnd 14 K3, *p12, k18, rep from * around, end last rep k15.
Rnd 15 (dec) *Yo, k2tog, yo, ssk, k9, k2tog, rep from * around—112 sts.
Rnd 16 Knit.
Rnd 17 (dec) *Yo, k2tog, yo, p2tog tbl, p8, p2tog, yo, k2tog, yo, ssk, k8, k2tog, rep from * around—104 sts.
Rnd 18 *K3, *p10, k16, rep from * around, end last rep k13.
Rnd 19 (dec) *Yo, k2tog, yo, ssk, k7, k2tog, rep from * around—96 sts.
Rnd 20 Knit.
Rnd 21 (dec) *Yo, k2tog, yo, p2tog tbl, p6, p2tog, yo, k2tog, yo, ssk, k6, k2tog, rep from * around—88 sts.
Rnd 22 K3, *p8, k14, rep from * around, end last rep k11.
Rnd 23 (dec) *Yo, k2tog, yo, ssk, k5, k2tog, rep from * around—80 sts.
Rnd 24 Knit.
Rnd 25 (dec) *Yo, k2tog, yo, p2tog tbl, p4, p2tog, yo, k2tog, yo, ssk, k4, k2tog, rep from * around—72 sts.
Rnd 26 K3, *p6, k12, rep from * around, end last rep k9.
Rnd 27 (dec) *Yo, k2tog, yo, ssk, k3, k2tog, rep from * around—64 sts.
Rnd 28 Knit.
Rnd 29 (dec) *Yo, k2tog, yo, p2tog tbl, p2, p2tog, yo, k2tog, yo, ssk, k2, k2tog, rep from * around—56 sts.
Rnd 30 K3, *p4, k10, rep from * around, end last rep K7.
Rnd 31 (dec) *Yo, k2tog, yo, ssk, k1, k2tog, rep from * around—48 sts.
Rnd 32 Knit.
Rnd 33 (dec) *Yo, k2tog, yo, ssk, k2tog, rep from * around—40 sts.
Rnd 34 Knit.
Rnd 35 (dec) *Yo, k2tog, yo, k3tog, rep from * around—32 sts.
Rnd 36 Knit.
Rnd 37 (dec) [K2tog] 16 times—16 sts.
Rnd 38 (dec) [K2tog] 8 times—8 sts.
Cut yarn, leaving a 6"/15cm tail. Thread tail through rem sts.

FAUX CABLED Hat

Paul Amato for lvarapresents.com

YOU'LL NEED:

YARN (4)
3½oz/100g or 140yd/130m of any worsted weight wool yarn.

NEEDLES
One set (5) size 8 (5mm) double-pointed needles (dpns) *or size to obtain gauge*

■■■■□

KNITTED MEASUREMENTS
Circumference at ribbing, slightly stretched 20"/51cm
Length 8"/20.5cm

GAUGES
18 sts and 24 rnds to 4"/10cm over pat st using size 8 (5mm) needles.
16 sts and 21 rnds over St st using size 8 (5mm) needles
Take time to check gauges.

STITCH GLOSSARY
3-st RT K3tog without slipping sts from LH needle, yo, k first st on LH needle once more, drop 3 sts just worked from LH needle.

S2KP Sl 2 sts tog as if to knit, k1, pass sl sts one at a time over the k1 to dec 2 sts.
Pattern stitch
Rnd 1 *3-st RT, p5; rep from * around.
Rnds 2–4 *K3, p5 rep from * around.
Rnd 5 Rep rnd 1.
Rnds 6–8 Rep rnds 2–4.
Rnd 9 Rep rnd 1.
Rnd 10 P4, *3-st RT, p5; rep from * to last 4 sts, 3-st RT, p1.
Rnds 11–13 *P4, k3, p1; rep from * around.
Rnd 14 Rep rnd 10.
Rnds 15–17 Rep rnds 11–13.
Rnd 18 Rep rnd 10.
K3, P1 Rib (multiple of 4 sts)
Rnd 1 *K3, p1; rep from * around.
Rep rnd 1 for k3, p1 rib.

HAT
Cast on 88 sts loosely. Join, taking care not to twist sts, and place marker for beg of rnd.
Work 8 rnds in k3, p1 rib.
Work rnds 1–18 in pat st.
Shape crown
Next (dec) rnd [3-st RT, p2tog, p1, p2tog] 11 times around—66 sts.
Next 3 rnds [K3, p3] 11 times around.
Next (dec) rnd [3-st RT, p3tog] 11 times around—44 sts.
Next 3 rnds [K3, p1] 11 times around.
Next (dec) rnd [S2KP, p1] 11 times around—22 sts.
Next rnd *K1, p1; rep from * around.
Next (dec) rnd [Ssk] 11 times around—11 sts.
Break yarn, leaving long tail. Thread tail through rem sts twice. Fasten off.

SNAIL Hat

Marcus Tuillis

YOU'LL NEED:

YARN ④
3½oz/100g (5¼oz/150g, 5¼oz/150g)
or 180yd/160m (270yd/240m,
270yd/240m) of any worsted weight
variegated wool yarn

NEEDLES
Two size 8 (5mm) double-pointed
needles (dpns)
or size to obtain gauge

KNITTED MEASUREMENTS
Sized for Small, Medium, Large. Shown in
size Small.
Circumference 18 (20, 22)"/45.5 (49.5, 56)
cm

GAUGE
22 sts and 30 rows to 4"/10cm over St st
using size 8 (5mm) needles.
Take time to check gauge.

CROWN
Cast on 4 sts and work in I-cord as foll:
Row 1 (RS) *K4, do not turn, sl sts back to
opposite end of needle, pull yarn tight;
rep from * for 1"/2.5cm. Turn work, place
marker.
Next row (WS) P4.
Next row (RS) Sl 1, k2, k1 tbl.
Next row P4.
Note The remainder of the hat is worked in
rows of St st. The first st of every RS row is
slipped as if to purl, forming the edge st.
Next row (RS) Sl 1, k2, sl 1, insert RH needle
under both strands of next st 4 rows
below, at base of I-cord. With LH needle, k
these 3 strands tog—4 sts. Rep last 4 rows
3 times more, working in each st of last
I-cord rnd.
Next row P4.
Next row Sl 1, k2, k1 tbl.
Next row P4. These 4 St st will begin to
curve around the base of the I-cord.
Connect the St sts as foll:
Next (joining) row Sl 1, k2, sl 1, insert RH
needle under both strands of the edge st
of the first St st row, with LH needle, k these
3 strands tog—4 sts. Cont to rep the last
4 rows, inserting RH needle under both
strands of every edge st of prev rnd, to continue inc'ing and spiraling until hat measures 8 (9, 10)"/20.5 (23, 25.5)cm in diameter.
If crown begins to ripple, inc less frequently
by skipping an occasional edge st.
Work the sides of the hat without inc'ing
by working every other RS row as a joining
row, picking up every other edge st. Work
for 4"/10cm.
Next rnd Dec for opening by working every
RS row as a joining row, cont to pick up
every other edge st.
Work 2 sts tog at the beg of every 6th row
until only 1 st rem. Cut yarn, pull through
last st to secure.

Brian Kraus, NYC; Bobb Connors

YOU'LL NEED:

YARN (4)
3½oz/100g or 170yd/150m of any
worsted weight wool blend yarn

NEEDLES
One pair size 10 (6mm) needles
or size to obtain gauge

ADDITIONAL MATERIALS
Size J/10 (6mm) crochet hook
Cable needle (cn)

KNITTED MEASUREMENTS
Circumference 19"/48.5cm

GAUGE
14 sts and 16 rows to 4"/10cm over cable
pats using size 10 (6mm) needles and 2
strands of yarn.
Take time to check gauge.

NOTE
Work with 2 strands of yarn held tog
throughout.

STITCH GLOSSARY
Cr2R Slip 1 st to cn and hold to *back*, k1, k1
from cn.
Cr2L Slip 1 st to cn and hold to *front*, k1, k1
from cn.
Cr3R Slip 1 st to cn and hold to *back*, k2, k1
from cn.
Cr3L Slip 2 sts to cn and hold to *front*, k1,
k2 from cn.
Cr4R Slip 2 sts to cn and hold to *back*, k2,
k2 from cn.

Cable #1 (over 8 sts)
Row 1 (RS) K4, Cr4R.

Rows 2, 4 and 6 Purl.
Row 3 K2, Cr4R, k2.
Row 5 Cr4R, k4.
Rep rows 1–6 for cable #1.

Cable #2 (over 4 sts)
Rows 1 and 3 (RS) Knit.
Rows 2, 4 and 6 Purl.
Row 5 Cr4R. Rep rows 1–6 for cable #2.

Cable #3 (over 8 sts)
Row 1 (RS) P2, Cr4R, p2.
Row 2 and all WS rows K the knit sts and p
the purl sts.
Row 3 P1, Cr3R, Cr3L, p1.
Row 5 Cr3R, k2, Cr3L.
Row 7 Cr3L, k2, Cr3R.
Row 9 P1, Cr3L, Cr3R, p1.
Row 10 Rep row 2.
Rep rows 1–10 for cable #3.

HAT
With 2 strands of yarn, cast on 66 sts. Work
in k1, p1 rib for 2 rows.
Beg cable pats
Next row (RS) *P2, work 8 sts cable #1, p2,
work 4 sts cable #2, p2, work 8 sts cable #3,
p2, work 4 sts cable #2; rep from * once
more, p2. Cont in pats as established, work
sts between cables in reverse St st, until

piece measures 4"/10cm from beg, end
with a WS row.
Top shaping
Next row (RS) Dec 1 st in each p2 section—57 sts. Work 3 rows even.
Next row (RS) Dec 2 sts in each cable section—41 sts. Work 3 rows even, keeping to
cable pat when possible, but working Cr2R
and Cr2L in place of 3- and 4-st cables.
Next row (RS) Dec 3 sts in each 6-st cable
section—29 sts. Work 1 row even. Dec 9
sts evenly on next row—20 sts. Work 1 row
even. K2tog across next row. Work 1 row
even. K2tog across next row. Cut yarn, leaving an end for sewing. Draw through rem 5
sts and pull tog tightly. Sew back seam.

FINISHING
With 2 strands held tog and crochet hook,
make two chains each approx 8"/20.5cm
long and attach to top of hat. Make two
1"/2.5cm pom-poms and sew to end of
each chain.

NEON Fair Isle

KNITTED MEASUREMENTS
Sized for Small, Medium/Large. Shown in size Small.
Circumference 18 (21¾)"/45.5 (55)cm
Length approx 9 (9½)"/23 (24)cm

GAUGES
16 sts and 24 rnds to 4"/10cm over St st using size 8 (5mm) needles.
20 sts and 24 rnds to 4"/10cm over St st and chart pat using size 9 (5.5mm) needles.
Take time to check gauge.

NOTE
When changing colors, twist yarns on WS to prevent holes in work. Carry colors not in use loosely across back of work.

CAP
With smaller needles and MC, cast on 77 (87) sts. Work in k1, p1 rib for 1"/2.5cm.
Inc row (RS) K2 (3), [kfb, k5 (3)] 12 (20) times, kfb, k2 (3)—90 (108) sts. Change to larger needles and cont in St st with MC for 3 rows.
Beg chart #1
Row 1 (RS) K0 (2) MC, work 15-st rep 6 (7) times, k0 (1) MC. Cont in pat as established, keeping first 2 sts and last st for size Medium/Large in MC, through row 5. With MC, work 3 rows in St st.
Beg chart #2
Row 1 (RS) Work 18-st rep 5 (6) times. Cont in pat as established through row 15. With MC, work 3 rows in St st.
Beg chart #3
Work 5 rows same as for chart #1. With MC, work 1 row in St st, dec 0 (8) sts evenly spaced across—90 (100) sts. Cont with MC only as foll:
Shape top
For size Medium/Large only
Next row (RS) [K8, k2tog] 10 times—(90) sts. P 1 row.
For both sizes
Next row (RS) [K7, k2tog] 10 times—80 sts. P 1 row.
Next row [K6, k2tog] 10 times—70 sts. P 1 row.
Next row [K5, k2tog] 10 times—60 sts. P 1 row.
Next row [K2, k2tog] 15 times—45 sts. P 1 row.
Next row [K1, k2tog] 15 times—30 sts. P 1 row.
Next row [K2tog] 15 times—15 sts.
Last row (WS) [P2tog] 7 times, p1. Cut yarn, leaving an end for sewing and draw through rem 8 sts.

FINISHING
Weave in ends. Block hat to measurements. Sew back seam.

YOU'LL NEED:

YARN ⑤
3½oz/100g or 140yd/130m of any bulky weight wool blend yarn in black (MC), shocking pink (A), acid green (B), and highlighter yellow (C)

NEEDLES
One pair each size 8 and 9 (5 and 5.5mm) needles
or size to obtain gauge

ADDITIONAL MATERIALS
Tapestry needle

CHART 1
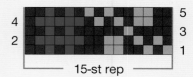
15-st rep

CHART 2
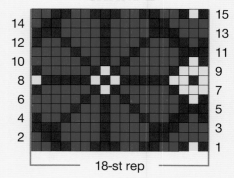
18-st rep

CHART 3
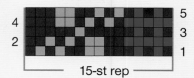
15-st rep

STITCH KEY
■ Black (MC)   ■ Shocking pink (A)
■ Acid green (B)
□ Highlighter yellow (C)

HOODED Scarf

Jack Deutsch

YOU'LL NEED:

YARN (4)
17½oz/500g or 950yd/870m of any worsted weight wool blend yarn

NEEDLES
One pair size 8 (5mm) needles
or size to obtain gauge

ADDITIONAL MATERIALS
Cable needle (cn)
Stitch markers

KNITTED MEASUREMENTS
Hood 10½" x 13½"/26.5cm x 34cm
Scarf 8½" x 60"/21.5cm x 152.5cm

GAUGES
19 sts and 26 rows to 4"/10cm over St st using size 8 (5mm) needles.
28 sts and 26 rows to 4"/10cm over chart A using size 8 (5mm) needles.
25 sts and 26 rows to 4"/10cm over chart B using size 8 (5mm) needles.
Take time to check gauges.

STITCH GLOSSARY
4-st LC Sl next 2 sts to cn and hold in *front*, k2, k2 from cn.
4-st RC Sl next 2 sts to cn and hold in *back*,

k2, k2 from cn.
4-st LPC Sl next 2 sts to cn and hold in *front*, p2, k2 from cn.
4-st RPC Sl next 2 sts to cn and hold in *back*, k2, p2 from cn.
K2, P2 RIB (multiple of 4 sts plus 2)
Row 1 (RS) K2, *p2, k2; rep from * to end.
Row 2 P2, *k2, p2; rep from * to end.
Rep rows 1 and 2 for k2, p2 rib.

SCARF (make 2 pieces)
Beg at bottom edge, cast on 54 sts. Work in k2, p2 rib for 4 rows.
Beg chart pats
Row 1 (RS) Work row 1 of chart A over 14 sts, pm, work row 1 of chart B over 26 sts, pm, work row 1 of chart C over 14 sts. Cont to foll charts A and C to row 4, then rep rows 1—4 to the end. AT THE SAME TIME, cont to foll chart B to row 34, then *rep rows 1—20 twice, then rows 21—34 once; rep from * once more, then rep rows 1—20 twice; piece should measure approx 30"/76cm from beg. Bind off in cable pat.

HOOD (make 2 pieces)
Beg at bottom edge, cast on 62 sts. Purl next row.
Beg chart pats
Row 1 (RS) Work row 1 of chart D over 18 sts, pm, work row 1 of chart B over 26 sts,

pm, work row 1 of chart E over 18 sts. Cont to foll charts D and E to row 4, then rep rows 1–4 to the end. AT THE SAME TIME, cont to foll chart B to row 34, then rep rows 1–20 twice. Beg with row 21, work even until piece measures 13"/33cm from beg, end with a WS row. Bind off in cable pat.

FINISHING
Sew bound-off edges of scarf pieces tog. Sew bound-off edges of hood pieces tog for top seam. Fold hood in half along top seam so RS are facing. Sew side edges of hood tog for back seam. Line up scarf seam with back seam of hood. Sew bottom edge of hood to edge of scarf.
Pompom
Make a 2½"/6.5cm diameter pompom and sew to peak of hood.

Stitch Key
☐ K on RS, P on WS
⊟ P on RS, K on WS
⊠ K tbl on RS, p tbl on WS
4-st LC
4-st RC
4-st LPC
4-st RPC

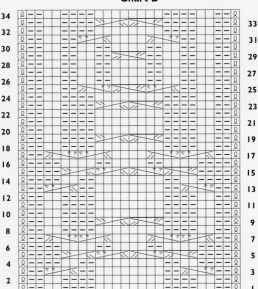

Chart B

26 sts

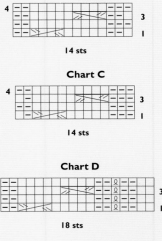

Chart A
14 sts

Chart C
14 sts

Chart D
18 sts

Chart E
18 sts

FAIR ISLE Cap

Eye[4]Media

YOU'LL NEED:

YARN ❷
1¾oz/50g or 120yd/110m of any sport weight wool yarn in citrus yellow (MC), orange (A), red (B), moss green (C), teal (D), and forest green (E)

NEEDLES
One set (4) size 6 (4mm) double-pointed needles (dpns)
or size to obtain gauge
Size 6 (4mm) circular needle, 16"/40cm long

KNITTED MEASUREMENTS
Circumference 19½"/49.5cm
Length 7"/18cm

GAUGE
26 sts and 30 rnds to 4"/10cm over St st foll chart using size 6 (4mm) needles.
Take time to check gauge.

NOTES
1 When changing colors foll chart, bring new yarn from underneath working yarn to avoid holes in work.
2 Cap is knit from the top and increased down to the lower edge.

CAP
Beg at center top of cap, with one size 6 (4mm) dpn and MC, cast on 8 sts.
Rnd 1 With needle 1, k2; with needle 2, k2; with needle 3, k2, k2tog (for 3 sts on needle 3) to join rnd. Join being careful that sts are not twisted. Pm to mark beg of rnd.
Rnd 2 *Yo, k1; rep from * 6 times more—14 sts.
Rnd 3 and all odd rnds Knit.
Rnd 4 *Yo, k2; rep from * 6 times more—21 sts.
Rnd 6 *Yo, k3; rep from * 6 times more—28 sts.
Rnd 8 *Yo, k4; rep from * 6 times more—35 sts.
Rnd 10 *Yo, k5; rep from * 6 times more—42 sts.
Rnd 12 *Yo, k6; rep from * 6 times more—49 sts.
Rnd 14 *Yo, k7; rep from * 6 times more—56 sts.
Rnd 16 *Yo, k8; rep from * 6 times more—63 sts.
Rnd 18 *Yo, k9; rep from * 6 times more—70 sts.

Rnd 20 *Yo, k10; rep from * 6 times more—77 sts.
Rnd 22 *Yo, k11; rep from * 6 times more—84 sts.
Rnd 23 Knit.
Note Change to circular needle for easier working. When foll chart as described, cont to foll the inc frequency every other rnd, always making the yo in the chart background color and work the new sts into the chart pat.
Beg chart
Rnd 1 Work chart rnd 1, *yo, k12; rep from * 6 times more—91 sts.
Rnds 2, 4, 6, 8, 10 Foll chart for color pat, knit.
Rnd 3 Foll chart, *yo, k13; rep from * 6 times more—98 sts.
Rnd 5 Foll chart, *yo, k14; rep from * 6 times more—105 sts.
Rnd 7 Foll chart, *yo, k15; rep from * 6 times more—112 sts.
Rnd 9 Foll chart, *yo, k16; rep from * 6 times more—119 sts.
Rnd 11 Foll chart, *yo, k17; rep from * 6 times more—126 sts. All incs are completed.
Rnd 12 *Cont 4-st rep of chart 4 times, work last 2 sts of chart; rep from * 6 times more. Cont in this way to foll chart until row 25 of chart is completed. With MC, k1 rnd.

BAND
Turn work to beg next rnd from WS of cap (that is, RS of band will be on the WS of the cap). Cont chart as established, work rnds 26–30 once. With E, purl 1 rnd (for turning ridge of band). Then foll chart, work rnds 26–30 once more. Bind off, leaving long end for sewing band in place.

FINISHING
Block cap flat. Turn up lower band to RS of cap along turning ridge. Carefully sew band in place through back lps of bound-off sts, matching st for st to cap's lower edge.

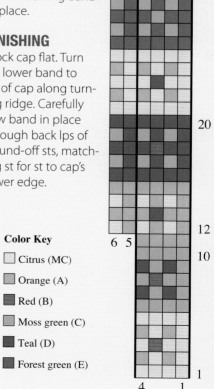

Color Key
☐ Citrus (MC)
▨ Orange (A)
▣ Red (B)
▨ Moss green (C)
▨ Teal (D)
▨ Forest green (E)

BUTTONED Cable Cap

YOU'LL NEED:

YARN (4)
3½oz/100g or 210yd/190m of any worsted weight cotton/wool blend yarn

NEEDLES
One each sizes 6 and 7 (4 and 4.5mm) circular needles, 16"/40cm long
or size to obtain gauge
Size 7 (4.5mm) double-pointed needles (dpns)

ADDITIONAL MATERIALS
Cable needle (cn)
Sixteen ½"/12mm buttons
Stitch marker

KNITTED MEASUREMENTS
Circumference (at brim) 21"/53.5 cm
Length 7¼"/18.5cm

GAUGE
20 sts and 28 rnds to 4"/10cm over St st using smaller needles.
Take time to check gauge.

STITCH GLOSSARY
6-st LC Sl 3 sts to cn and hold to *front*, k3, k3 from cn.

CABLED BRIM
With smaller needle, cast on 128 sts, place marker (pm) and join for working in the round, taking care not to twist sts.
Rnd 1 *K2, p2; rep from * around. Rep rnd 1 for k2, p2 rib and work 1 rnd more.
Next (buttonhole) rnd *K2, p1, yo, k2tog, k1, p2; rep from * around. Work 2 rnds in

k2, p2 rib. Change to larger needle.
Next 2 rnds *K6, p2; rep from * around.
Beg chart pat
Rnd 1 Work 8-st rep 16 times around. Work rnds 1–6 of chart 3 times. Rep rnd 1 once more.
Next (dec) rnd *K5, ssk, k2tog, k4, ssk, p1; rep from * around—104 sts. Piece measures approx 3½"/9cm from beg. Purl one rnd for turning ridge. Change to smaller needle and work in St st (k every rnd) for 1"/2.5cm.

BODY
Turn work inside out so WS is facing, cont in St st until piece measures 6"/15cm from turning ridge.
Note A small hole will result at the beg of the rnd from changing directions when you turn the work inside out. This hole will be covered by the brim.
Shape crown
Note Change to dpns when sts no longer fit comfortably on circular needle.
Rnd 1 *K11, k2tog; rep from * around—96 sts.
Rnd 2, 4, 6, 8 and 10 Knit.
Rnd 3 *K10, k2tog; rep from * around—88 sts.
Rnd 5 *K9, k2tog; rep from * around—80 sts.
Rnd 7 *K8, k2tog; rep from * around—72 sts.
Rnd 9 *K7, k2tog; rep from * around—64 sts.
Rnd 11 *K6, k2tog; rep from * around—56 sts. Cont to dec 8 sts every rnd, working 1 less st before each k2tog, until 16 sts rem.
Next rnd *K2tog; rep from * around —

8 sts. Cut yarn and thread through rem sts.

FINISHING
Turn up brim and sew on buttons to correspond to buttonholes.

STITCH KEY
☐ k on RS
⊟ p on RS
▨ 6-st LC

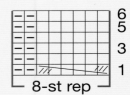

8-st rep

FRENCH Connection

YOU'LL NEED:

YARN (4)
1¾oz/50g or 130yd/120m of any worsted weight wool yarn in light green (A). 1¾oz/50g or 100yd/90m of any worsted weight wool/mohair blend yarn in light green (B)

NEEDLES
One set (5) double-pointed needles (dpns) size 11 (8mm)
or size to obtain gauge
Size 10 (6mm) circular needle, 24"/60cm long

ADDITIONAL MATERIALS
Size I/9 (5.5mm) crochet hook
Stitch marker
One 12"/30.5cm round dinner plate

■■■□

KNITTED MEASUREMENTS
Diameter before felting 12"/30.5cm
Diameter after felting 10½"/27cm

GAUGE
12 sts and 16 rnds to 4"/10cm over pat st using size 11 (8mm) needle and 1 strand A and B held tog (before felting).
Take time to check gauge.

STITCH GLOSSARY
Pattern Stitch (multiple of 4 sts)
Rnd 1 *K2, p2; rep from * around.
Rnds 2 and 4 K the knit sts and p the purl sts.
Rnd 3 *P2, k2; rep from * around.
Rep rnds 1–4 for pat st.

NOTE
Beret is worked in the round with 1 strand of A and B held tog throughout.

BERET
Beg at top center, with 1 strand A and B held tog, and size I/9 (5.5mm) crochet hook, ch 4, join with sl st to form ring.
Rnd 1 Using crochet hook to pull loops through ch ring, pull up 8 loops in ring and place evenly divided onto 4 dpn, taking care not to twist sts. Pm to mark beg of rnd.
Rnd 2 K1 into front and back of each st around—16 sts.
Rnd 3 [K1, inc 1 st in next st] 8 times—24 sts.
Rnd 4 Purl.
Rnd 5 [K2, inc 1 st in next st] 8 times—32 sts.
Rnd 6 [K3, inc 1 st in next st] 8 times—40 sts.
Rnd 7 [K4, inc 1 st in next st] 8 times—48 sts.
Rnd 8 Purl.
Rnd 9 [K5, inc 1 st in next st] 8 times—56 sts.
Rnd 10 [K6, inc 1 st in next st] 8 times—64 sts.
Rnd 11 [K7, inc 1 st in next st] 8 times— 72 sts.
Rnd 12 Purl.
Rnd 13 [K11, inc 1 st in next st] 6 times—78 sts.
Rnd 14 [K12, inc 1 st in next st] 6 times—84 sts.
Rnd 15 Knit.
Rnds 16 and 17 [K2, p2] 21 times.
Rnds 18 and 19 [P2, k2] 21 times.
Rep rnds 16–19 a total of 3 more times. Then rep rnds 16 and 17 once.
Change to size 10 (6mm) circular needle.
Next rnd *K2, p2, k2tog, k1, p2, k2, p2tog, p1; rep from * around—72 sts.
Work even in k2, p2 rib for 7 more rnds.

Last rnd *K2, p2tog; rep from * around—54 sts. Bind off.

FELTING
Step 1 Immerse beret in water, then roll in a towel to remove excess water. Using a 12"/30.5cm dinner plate, let beret dry while stretched over plate.
Step 2 Using low level, hot water setting and delicate cycle, place beret in standard washing machine with ½ measure of detergent. Put through wash cycle. Place beret in clothes dryer on normal setting and put through dry cycle.

SNOWFLAKE Beret

Eye[4]Media

KNITTED MEASUREMENTS
Circumference 19"/48cm
Diameter 10"/25.5cm

GAUGE
18 sts and 28 rows/rnds to 4"/10cm over St st using larger circular needles.
Take time to check gauge.

BERET
With smaller circular needle, cast on 96 sts loosely. Join being careful not to twist sts on needle and pm to mark beg of rnd.
Rnd 1 *K1 tbl, p1; rep from * around.
Rep rnd 1 for twisted k1, p1 rib for 4 rnds more.
Next (inc) rnd Cont in twisted rib as established, work as foll: *rib 2 sts, M1 purlwise, [rib 3 sts, M1 purlwise] twice, rib 2 sts, M1 purlwise, rib 3 sts, M1 purlwise, rib 3 sts; rep from * 5 times more—126 sts. Change to larger circular needle.

Beg chart pat
Set-up rnd Remove marker, *k4, (replace marker for new beg of rnd), p6, k1 tbl, p6, k4; rep from * (without markers) 5 times more. Then working 21-st rep 6 times, work rnds 1–9 of chart 3 times.

Shape crown
Changing to dpn when there are too few sts to fit on circular needle, work rnds 1–29 of chart—6 sts rem. Pull yarn through rem 6 sts and draw up tightly and secure.

FINISHING
Wash finished beret in lukewarm water and mild soap. Wring out water gently. Insert a 10"/25.5cm plate into beret and allow to dry.

Embroidery
Working into 3 alternating 8-st St st segments, embroider 2 snowflakes in each of these segments in lazy daisy st foll embroidery chart.

Tassel
Wind yarn 25 times around a 4"/10cm piece of cardboard. Set aside for tassel.

Braid
Cut 6 strands of yarn 15"/38cm long. Using tapestry needle, draw these strands through wrapped yarn at top of cardboard. Using 2 strands of yarn for each section, braid yarn tightly. Cut a 10"/26cm piece of yarn and wrap tightly around tassel strands at approx 1"/2.5cm from top end of tassel. Cut other cord to form tassel. Trim tassel and fasten with braid to top of beret.

Embroidery Chart

Stitch Key
☐ K on RS, p on WS
⊟ P on RS, k on WS
Ⓠ K1tbl
⊠ Ssk
⊠ K2tog
⬔ Slip one st to cn and hold to *back*, k1tbl, p1 from cn
⬔ Slip one st to cn and hold to *front*, p1, k1tbl, k1 from cn
■ No stitch

21-st rep

29 27 25 23 21 19 17 15 13 11 9 7 5 3 1

21 19 17 15 13 11 9 7 5 3 1

SLOUCHY Beret

YOU'LL NEED:

YARN
7oz/200g or 220yd/200m of any
bulky weight wool blend yarn.

NEEDLES
One size 10 (6mm) circular needle,
24"/60cm long
or size to obtain gauge
One set (5) size 10 (6mm) double-
pointed needles (dpns)
One size 9 (4.5mm) circular needle
16"/40cm long

ADDITIONAL MATERIALS
Stitch markers

Paul Amato for Harepresents.com

KNITTED MEASUREMENTS
Circumference (at brim) 18"/45.5cm
Length 10"/25.5cm

GAUGE
12 sts and 23 rnds to 4"/10cm over double
seed st using larger needle.
Take time to check gauge.

STITCH GLOSSARY
kfb Inc 1 st by k into front and back of next st.
Seed Stitch (over an odd number of sts)
Rnd 1 *K1, p1; rep from * around.
Rnd 2 P the knit sts and k the purl sts.
Rep rnd 2 for seed st.
**Double Seed Stitch (over an odd number
of sts)**
Rnds 1 and 2 *K1, p1; rep from * to last st, k1.
Rnds 3 and 4 *P1, k1; rep from * to last st, p1.

NOTE
Hat is worked from the top down. Change
to circular needle when there are too many
sts to fit comfortably on dpns.

HAT
With dpns, cast on 9 sts and join, being
careful not to twist sts. Place marker (pm)
to mark beg of rnds and slip marker every
rnd. K 1 rnd.
**Next (inc) rnd K1, *kfb; rep from *
around—17 sts. Work 4 rounds in seed st.**
Rep between **'s twice more—65 sts.

Next (inc) rnd K1, [kfb] 28 times, k8, [kfb] 28
times—121 sts. Place a new marker in this
rnd but do not slip it on the following rnds.
Work in double seed st until hat measures
6"/15cm from new marker, end with a rnd
1. Change to smaller circular needle.
Next (dec) rnd [K2tog, p2tog] 13 times,

k2tog, [k1, p1] 7 times, k1, [p2tog, k2tog] 13
times—68 sts.
Brim
Work in k1, p1 rib for 2"/5cm. Bind off
loosely in rib.

TASSELED Earflap Hat

KNITTED MEASUREMENTS
Circumference 19 (22)"/48.5 (56)cm

GAUGE
8 sts and 12 rnds to 4"/10cm over St st using size 15 (10mm) needles.
Take time to check gauge.

EARFLAP ONE
With 2 dpns, cast on 3 sts. Work in St st for 2 rows.
Row 3 (inc RS) K1, M1, k1, M1, k1—5 sts.
Row 4 Purl. Row 5 (inc) K1, M1, k3, M1, k1—7 sts.
Row 6 Purl.
Row 7 K1, M1, k5, M1, k1—9 sts.
Row 8 Purl. Cut yarn, leaving a 6"/15cm tail. Set piece aside.

EARFLAP TWO
Work as for Earflap One, without cutting yarn at end of last row. Cast on 4 (5) sts at right side of earflap, change to circular needle.

HAT BODY
Note Change to dpn when sts no longer fit comfortably on circular needle.
Rnd 1 (joining) K across 4 (5) cast-on sts, 9 sts of Earflap Two, cast on 12 (16) sts (front of hat), knit across 9 sts of Earflap One, cast on 4 (5) sts—38 (44) sts. Place marker for end of rnd, join for knitting in the round, taking care not to twist sts.
Rnds 2–11 Knit.
Rnd 12 (dec) K1, k2tog, k to last 3 sts, ssk, k1—36 (42) sts.
Rnds 13–14 Knit.
Rnd 15 *K4 (5), k2tog; rep from * around—32 (36) sts.
Rnds 16–17 Knit.
Rnd 18 *K3 (4), k2tog; rep from * around—24 (30) sts.
Rnds 19–20 Knit.
Rnd 21 *K2 (3), k2tog; rep from * around—18 (24) sts.
Rnds 22–23 Knit.
Rnd 24 *K1 (2), k2tog; rep from * around—12 (18) sts.
Rnd 25 Knit
Rnd 26 *K0 (1), k2tog; rep from * around—6 (12) sts.
Rnd 27 Knit.
For Large Size Only
Rnd 28 *K2tog; rep from * to marker—6 sts.
Rnd 29 Knit.
For All Sizes
Cut yarn, leaving an 8"/20.5cm tail, thread through rem sts and cinch tightly to close.

FINISHING
Edging
With crochet hook and RS facing, attach yarn to center back st, ch 1, sc evenly around lower edge of hat and earflaps, working loosely to allow for stretch. Join with sl st to beg st, fasten off and weave in ends.
Ties (make 2)
With crochet hook, attach yarn at point of earflap and chain to 12"/30.5cm (or desired length). Fasten off. Tie ends of chain in knot and bury tails in knot.
Tassel
Wrap yarn around 7"/18cm piece of cardboard 8 times. With separate 16"/40.5cm length of yarn, tie strands together at one end of wrap. Cut strands at opposite end. With a 24"/61cm length of yarn, starting 1"/2.5cm below tied end, wrap yarn around strands a few times, then tie off burying tails in center of tassel. Attach to point of hat securely and weave in tails.

CANDY STRIPES

YOU'LL NEED:

YARN (5)
3½oz/100g of any bulky weight cotton blend yarn in pink (A)
1¾oz/50g in white (B), orange (C), and dark pink (D)

NEEDLES
One pair size 9 (5.5mm) needles
or size to obtain gauge

ADDITIONAL MATERIALS
Size I/9 (5.5mm) crochet hook

KNITTED MEASUREMENTS
Circumference approx 21"/53cm
Length 11"/28cm

GAUGE
15 sts and 22 rows to 4"/10cm over St st using size 9 (5.5mm) needles.
Take time to check gauge.

HAT
With D, cast on 86 sts. K 4 rows. Change to A.
Next row (RS) K1, *k26, k2tog; rep from * to last st, k1. Work 3 rows even. Rep last 4 rows twice more, working 1 less k st between decs every dec row—77 sts. Change to D. K 2 rows. Change to B.
Next row (RS) K1, *k23, k2tog; rep from * to last st, k1. Work 3 rows even. Rep last 4 rows twice more, working 1 less k st between decs every dec row—68 sts. Change to D. K 2 rows. Change to C.
Next row (RS) K1, *k20, k2tog; rep from * to last st, k1. Work 3 rows even. Rep last 4 rows twice more, working 1 less k st between decs every dec row—59 sts. Change to D. K 2 rows. Change to A.
Next row (RS) K1, k2tog, *k7, k2tog; rep from * to last 2 sts, k2tog. Work 3 rows even. Rep last 4 rows twice more, working 1 less k st between decs every dec row—35 sts. Change to D. K 2 rows. Change to B.
Next row (RS) K1, k2tog, *k4, k2tog; rep

from * to last 2 sts, k2tog. Work 3 rows even. Rep last 4 rows twice more, working 1 less k st between decs every dec row—14 sts.
Next row (RS) K2tog across—7 sts.
Cut yarn, leaving a long tail for sewing seam. Draw through rem sts and fasten tightly. Sew back seam.

EAR FLAPS
With WS facing and B, pick up and k16 sts, beg 2½"/6.5cm from back seam.
Note Read foll instructions before beg to work. Working in garter st, work stripe pat as foll: *2 rows B, 2 rows C, 2 rows B, 2 rows

A; rep from * twice more, work 2 rows B, AT SAME TIME, dec 1 st each side every other row beg with 2nd B stripe—4 sts and 26 rows. Bind off. Work a 2nd ear flap in same way along other side of back seam.

FINISHING
With RS facing, crochet hook and D, work 1 rnd sc around lower edge and ear flaps.
With 2 strands of D held tog, make 4 braids approx 5"/12.5cm long and attach to ends of ear flaps.
With all colors held tog, make 3"/7.5cm pompom. Attach to top of hat.

BLUE BAYOU

Quenet

YOU'LL NEED:

YARN
3½oz/100g or 100yd/90m of any bulky weight wool yarn in blue (MC) and brown (CC)

NEEDLES
One set (4) size 11 (8mm) needles
or size to obtain gauge

ADDITIONAL MATERIALS
Size L/11 (8mm) crochet hook
Cable needle (cn)
Stitch markers

KNITTED MEASUREMENTS
Sized for Infant (Toddler, Child, Adult Small, Adult Large)
Circumference 12 (14, 16, 18, 20)"/30.5 (35.5, 40.5, 45.5, 50.5)cm
Length approx 9 (9, 11, 11, 11½)"/23 (23, 28, 28, 29) cm

GAUGE
14 sts and 14 rows to 4"/10cm over cable pat using size 11 (8mm) needles.
Take time to check gauge.

STITCH GLOSSARY
6-St RC Sl 3 sts to cn and hold to *back*, k3, k3 from cn.
6-St dec RC Sl 3 sts to cn and hold to *back*, k1, k2tog; then work ssk, k1 from cn.
4-St RC Sl 2 sts to cn and hold to *back*, k2, k2 from cn.
4-St dec RC Sl 2 sts to cn and hold to *back*, k2tog; then work ssk from cn.

HAT
With MC, cast on 42 (49, 56, 63, 70) sts. Divide sts evenly over 3 needles. Pm and join, being careful not to twist sts.
Rnd 1 (RS) *P1, k6; rep from * to end.
Rnds 2–5 K the knit and p the purl sts.
Rnd 6 *P1, 6-st RC; rep from * to end.
Rnds 7–13 K the knit and p the purl sts.
Rnd 14 Rep rnd 6.
Rnds 15–19 K the knit and p the purl sts.

Rnd 20 (dec rnd) *P1, 6-st dec RC; rep from * around—30 (35, 40, 45, 50) sts.
Rnds 21–25 K the knit and p the purl sts.
Rnd 26 *(sizes Child, Adult Small, Adult Large only)* *P1, 4-st RC; rep from * around.
Rnds 27–29 *(sizes Child, Adult Small, Adult Large only)* K the knit and p the purl sts.
Rnd 30 *(dec rnd for all sizes)* *P1, 4-st dec RC; rep from * around—18 (21, 24, 27, 30) sts. Work even for 3 (3, 5, 5, 6) rnds more.
Next dec rnd *P1, k2tog; rep from * around—12 (14, 16, 18, 20) sts.
Next dec rnd *K2tog; rep from * around— 6 (7, 8, 9, 10) sts.

FINISHING
Cut yarn and pull through rem sts. Draw up tightly to secure. Fasten off.

I-cord edging
With RS facing, dpn and CC, pick up and k 1 st in each cast-on st around lower edge. With CC and 2nd dpn, cast on 3 sts.
Rnd 1 *K2, sl 1, k1 from picked up edge of hat, psso to join I-cord to edge. Slide sts to beg of same dpn; rep from * until all sts are worked. Bind off. Sew cast-on and bound-off edges of I-cord tog.

Tassel
With MC and CC, make 6"/15cm long tassel. With MC and crochet hook chain 2"/5cm. Attach to top of hat, then attach tassel to end of chain.

MOUNTAIN Lodge Hat

Eye[4]Media

KNITTED MEASUREMENTS
Circumference 20½"/52cm
Length (excluding cinched top) 10"/25.5cm

GAUGE
22 sts and 26 rows to 4"/10cm over St st foll charts using larger needles.
Take time to check gauge.

NOTE
When changing colors, bring new yarn from underneath working yarn to avoid holes in work.

HAT
Beg at lower edge with smaller needles and MC, cast on 106 sts.
Row 1 (WS) Knit.
Row 2 With A, k2, * with B, k2, with A, k2; rep from * to end.
Row 3 With A, p2, * with B, k2, with A, p2; rep from * to end.
Row 4 With A, k2, *with B, p2, with A, k2; rep from * to end.
Rep rows 3 and 4 for 2-color rib once more. Then rep row 3 once. Change to larger needles. With C, k1 row, p1 row. With B, k2 rows. With C, k1 row.

Next row (WS) With C, purl, inc 6 sts evenly spaced across—112 sts.
Beg chart 1
Row 1 (RS) Foll row 1 of chart 1, work 8-st rep 14 times across. Cont to foll chart 1 through row 15.
Next row (WS) With C, purl, dec 6 sts evenly spaced across—106 sts. With C, k1 row, p1 row. With D, k2 rows.
Beg chart 2
Row 1 (RS) Beg with st 1 of row 1, work to end of row, then work 4-st rep across row 25 times more. Cont to foll chart 2 through row 5. With C, p2 rows.
Beg chart 3
Row 1 (WS) With MC, foll row 1 of chart 3, purl. Cont to foll chart 3, purl. Cont to foll chart 3, working rows 2–5 and working 2-st rep across. With A, k2 rows
Beg chart 4
Row 1 (RS) Beg with st 1 of row 1, work even with C across. Cont to foll chart 4, working 2-st rep 53 times across, through row 10.
Shape top
Row 1 (RS) With MC, k3, [k2tog, k8] 10 times, k3—96 sts.
Row 2 With MC, knit.
Row 3 With C, k3, [k2tog, k7] 10 times, k3—86 sts.
Row 4 With C, purl.
Row 5 With B, k3, [k2tog, k6] 10 times, k3—76 sts.
Row 6 With B, purl.
Row 7 With D, k3, [k2tog, k5] 10 times, k3—66 sts.
Row 8 With D, knit.
Row 9 With C, k3, [k2tog, k4] 10 times, k3—56 sts.
Row 10 With A, purl.
Row 11 With A, k3, [k2tog, k3] 10 times, k3—46 sts.
With A, [p1 row, k1 row] twice. With B, [k1 row, p1 row] 3 times.
Beg chart 5
Row 1 (RS) Work 2-st rep of row 1 of chart 5 23 times across. Work row 2 of chart 5. With C, knit 1 row. With C, bind off knitwise on WS, leaving a long end for sewing back seam.

YOU'LL NEED:
YARN ④
Classic Wool by Patons, 3½oz/100g, 223yd/204m, wool
1 ball each in orange (MC), gold (A), #213 blue (B), green (C) and red (D)

NEEDLES
One pair each sizes 6 and 7 (4 and 4.5mm) needles
or size to obtain gauge

FINISHING
Sew back seam. Block hat flat.
Twisted cord
Cut 6 strands A and 5 strands D each 20"/51cm long. Using the 2 colors, make a twisted cord by holding one set of ends by one person and the other set of ends by another person. Each person should twist the ends to their right until the cord begins to curl. The cord will twist around itself. Knot both ends. Tie cord around top of hat around the A color band as shown in photo.

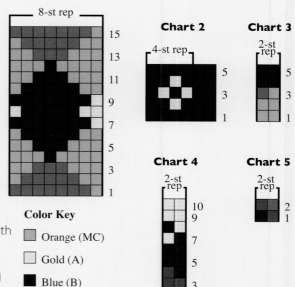

Chart I
8-st rep
15
13
11
9
7
5
3
1

Chart 2
4-st rep
5
3
1

Chart 3
2-st rep
5
3
1

Chart 4
2-st rep
10
9
7
5
3
1

Chart 5
2-st rep
2
1

Color Key
Orange (MC)
Gold (A)
Blue (B)
Green (C)
Red (D)

MOSAIC Hat

Quenet

YOU'LL NEED:

YARN (5)
3½oz/100g or 85yd/75m of any bulky weight wool blend yarn in purple (A) and pink (B)

NEEDLES
One set (5) size 10½ (6.5mm) double-pointed needles (dpns)

ADDITIONAL MATERIALS
Stitch markers

KNITTED MEASUREMENTS
Circumference 20"/51cm
Length 8"/20.5cm

GAUGE
13 sts and 21 rows to 4"/10cm over sl st pat using size 10½ (6.5mm) dpns.
Take time to check gauge.

STITCH GLOSSARY
Slip Stitch Pattern (multiple of 14 sts)
Rnd 1 With A, *k1, sl 1, k3, sl 1, k1; rep from * around.
Rnd 2 and all even rnds With color used in previous rnd, k the knit sts and sl the slipped sts.
Rnd 3 With B, *sl 1, k3, sl 1, k4, sl 1, k3, sl 1; rep from * around.
Rnd 5 With A, *k3, sl 1, k3; rep from * around.
Rnd 7 With B, *k2, sl 1, k3, sl 2, k3, sl 1, k2; rep from * around.
Rnd 8 Rep rnd 2.
Rep rnds 1–8 for sl st pat.

NOTES
1 When working sl st pat, always sl sts purlwise with yarn in back.
2 Work garter st in the rnd as foll: *k 1 rnd, p 1 rnd; rep from * for garter st in the rnd.

HAT
With A, cast on 70 sts. Divide over 3 dpn as foll: 23 sts on 1st needle, 23 sts on 2nd needle, 24 sts on 3rd needle. Pm and join, taking care not to twists st on needle. P 1 rnd with A. Then work garter st band as foll: 2 rnds B, 2 rnds A, 2 rnds B. Work rnds 1–8 of sl st pat once, then work rnds 1–6 once more. Then beg with rnd 3, work sl st pat in reverse as foll: work rnds 3–1, then cont to rep rnds 8–1 until 30 rnds of sl st pat have been worked above garter st band.

Shape crown
Next (dec) rnd *Work 5 sts in pat, k2tog, ssk, work 5 sts in pat; rep from * to end—60 sts. Work 1 rnd even.
Next (dec) rnd *Work 4 sts in pat, k2tog, ssk, work 4 sts in pat; rep from * to end—50 sts. Work 1 rnd even.
Next (dec) rnd Work 3 sts in pat, k2tog, ssk, work 3 sts in pat; rep from * to end—40 sts. Work 1 rnd even.
Next (dec) rnd *Work 2 sts in pat, k2tog, ssk, work 2 sts in pat; rep from * to end—30 sts. Work 1 rnd even.
Next (dec) rnd *Work 1 st in pat, k2tog, ssk, work 1 st in pat; rep from * to end—20 sts. Work 1 rnd even.
Next (dec) rnd *K2tog, ssk; rep from * to end—10 sts.
Cut yarn. Draw through rem sts and fasten tightly.

SIMPLE Stripes

YOU'LL NEED:

YARN
1¾oz/50g or 80yd/70m of any
worsted weight wool or wool blend
yarn in pink, turquoise, orange,
white, and lime.

NEEDLES
One set (5) each size 7 and 8 (4.5
and 5mm) double-pointed needles
(dpns) *or size to obtain gauge*

ADDITIONAL MATERIALS
One size K-10½ (6.5mm) crochet
hook
Tapestry needle

Paul Amato for lvarepresents.com

KNITTED MEASUREMENTS
Sized for Baby (Child, Adult)
Circumference 16 (18, 20)"/40.5 (45.5, 51cm
Length (without earflaps) 7½ (7¾, 8)"/19 (19.5, 20.5)cm

GAUGE
18 sts and 26 rows to 4"/10cm over St st
using larger needles.
Take time to check gauge.

STITCH GLOSSARY
Stripe Pattern
2 rnds each lime, white, orange, pink, and
turquoise.
Rep these 10 rnds for Stripe Pattern.

HAT
With smaller needles and turquoise, cast
on 64 (72, 80) sts. Place marker for begin-
ning of rnd and join for knitting in the
round, taking care not to twist sts. Knit 1
rnd turquoise, then work in garter st and
stripe pat for 16 rnds. Work one rnd in pink,
then in next pink rnd inc 8 (9, 10) sts evenly
across rnd—72 (81, 90) sts.
Switch to larger needles and St st, work 20
rnds. Working in Stripe Pat, dec as foll:
Adult Size only
Next rnd *K2tog, k8; rep from * to end. K 1 rnd.
Adult and Child Sizes only
Next rnd *K2tog, k7; rep from * to end. K 1 rnd.

All Sizes
Next rnd *K2tog, k6; rep from * to end. K 1 rnd.
Next rnd *K2tog, k5; rep from * to end. K 1 rnd.
Next rnd *K2tog, k4; rep from * to end. K 1 rnd.
Next rnd *K2tog, k3; rep from * to end. K 1 rnd.
Next rnd *K2tog, k2; rep from * to end. K 1 rnd.
Next rnd *K2tog, k1; rep from * to end. K 1 rnd.
Next rnd *K2tog; rep from * to end. Cut
long tail of yarn, thread through rem sts,
cinch to close.

EARFLAPS
Mark beg of cast-on edge as center back.
With RS facing, larger needles and hot pink,
beg at 8th (9th, 11th) st to the left of center
back and pick up 16 sts along cast-on
edge. Knit 1 row. Working stripe pattern in
white, lime, turquoise, pink, orange.
Continue in pat and dec 1 st each side
every WS row 7 times, end with first row of
turquoise—2 sts rem. Bind off.
Rep on right side of hat for second earflap.

CROCHET EDGING
With crochet hook and natural, beg at
center back of hat and work 1 sc in every st
along cast on row and in every other row
along ear flaps. Fasten off.

BABY'S Earflap Hat

YOU'LL NEED:

YARN ⓷
1¾oz/50g of any DK weight wool yarn in red (A) and coral (B) OR purple (A) and aqua (B)

NEEDLES
One pair size 6 (4mm) needles
or size to obtain gauge

ADDITIONAL MATERIALS
Size G/6 (4.5mm) crochet hook
Stitch markers

KNITTED MEASUREMENTS
Circumference 17"/43cm
Length (excluding earflaps) 5½"/14cm

GAUGE
19 sts and 28 rows to 4"/10cm over St st using size 6 (4mm) needles.
Take time to check gauge.

CAP
Beg at lower edge with A, cast on 80 sts. Work in St st for 5"/12.5cm.
Top shaping
Next row (RS) *K6, k2tog; rep from * to end—70 sts. **Next row** Purl.
Next row *K5, k2tog; rep from * to end—60 sts. **Next row** Purl. **Next row** *K4, k2tog, rep from * to end—50 sts. **Next row** Purl.
Next row *K3, k2tog; rep from * to end—40 sts. **Next row** Purl. **Next row** *K2, k2tog; rep from * to end—30 sts. **Next row** Purl.
Next row *K1, k2tog; rep from * to end—20 sts. **Next row** Purl. **Next row** *K2tog; rep from * to end—10 sts.
Cut yarn leaving long end for sewing seam and pull through rem sts and draw up tightly to secure. Sew back seam and fasten off.
Block cap flat.
Earflaps
Place 2 markers either side of center front 20 sts of cap. Pm at 18 sts to the left and 18 sts to the right of these 2 markers. Working from RS, with B, pick up and k one set of 18 sts for one earflap.
Row 1 (WS) With B, purl.
Row 2 (RS) With B, knit, dec 1 st each side of row—16 sts. **Row 3** With B, purl.
Row 4 With A, knit, dec 1 st each side of row—14 sts.
Rows 5 and 7 With A, purl.
Row 6 With A, knit. **Row 8** With B, knit, dec 1 st each side of row—12 sts.
Rows 9 and 11 With B, purl.
Row 10 With B, knit, dec 1 st each side of row—10 sts. **Row 12** With A, knit, dec 1 st each side of row—8 sts. **Row 13** With A, purl. **Row 14** With A, knit, dec 1 st each side of row—6 sts. On next WS row, bind off 6 sts. Work other earflap in same way.
With crochet hook and B, join with a sl st and beg at center back seam, *work 1 sc in each st along lower edge, 11 sts along side of one earflap, 6 sts across lower edge of earflap, 11 sts along other side of earflap; rep from * once, work 1 sc in each sc to end. Join with a sl st to first sc and fasten off.
Twisted cords (make 2)
Cut 1 strand each of A and B 30"/76cm long. Make a twisted cord and attach with a knot pulled through from WS at sc edge.
Pompom
With A and B, make a 2"/5cm pompom. Trim pompom and fasten to top of cap.

CABLED Brim

YOU'LL NEED:

YARN (4)
4oz/113g or 230yd/210m of any worsted weight wool yarn in magenta (A) and variegated pink (B)

NEEDLES
One pair size 7 (4.5mm) needles
or size to obtain gauge
Size 7 (4.5mm) circular needle, 16"/40.5cm long
One set (4) size 7 (4.5mm) double-pointed needles (dpns)

ADDITIONAL MATERIALS
Cable needle (cn)
Stitch marker

KNITTED MEASUREMENTS
Circumference 22"/56cm

GAUGE
22 sts and 28 rows to 4"/10cm over St st using size 7 (4.5mm) needles.
Take time to check gauge.

NOTE
Cabled brim is worked back and forth in rows and the crown is worked in rnds.

STITCH GLOSSARY
4-st RPC Sl next st to cn and hold in *back*, k3, p1 from cn.
4-st LPC Sl next 3 sts to cn and hold in *front*, p1, k3 from cn.
7-st RPC Sl next 4 sts to cn and hold in *back*, k3, sl last st on cn to LH needle and p it, k3 from cn.
MB (bobble) In same st work k1, [p1, k1] twice; turn, k5; turn, p5; pass the 2nd, 3rd, 4th, then 5th sts over the first st.
Double Moss Stitch (multiple of 4 sts)
Rnds 1 and 2 *K2, p2; rep from * around.
Rnds 3 and 4 *P2, k2; rep from * around.
Rep rnds 1–4 for double moss st.

HAT
Cabled brim
With straight needles and A, cast on 19

sts using a provisional cast-on (optional).
Row 1 (WS) P2, k4, p3, k1, p3, k4, sl last 2 sts to RH needle purlwise.
Row 2 K2, p4, 7-st RPC, p4, sl last 2 sts to RH needle purlwise.
Row 3 Rep row 1.
Row 4 K2, p3, 4-st RPC, p1, 4-st LPC, p3, sl last 2 sts to RH needle purlwise.
Row 5 P2, k3, p3, k3, p3, k3, sl last 2 sts to RH needle purlwise.
Row 6 K2, p2, 4-st RPC, p3, 4-st LPC, p2, sl last 2 sts to RH needle purlwise.
Row 7 P2, k2, p3, k5, p3, k2, sl last 2 sts to RH needle purlwise.
Row 8 K2, p2, k3, p2, MB, p2, k3, p2, sl last 2 sts to RH needle purlwise.
Row 9 Rep row 7.
Row 10 K2, p2, 4-st LPC, p3, 4-st RPC, p2, sl last 2 sts to RH needle purlwise.
Row 11 Rep row 5.
Row 12 K2, p3, 4-st LPC, p1, 4-st RPC, p3, sl last 2 sts to RH

needle purlwise.
Row 13 Rep row 1.
Row 14 Rep row 2.
Row 15 Rep row 1.
Row 16 Rep row 4.
Row 17 Rep row 5.
Row 18 Rep row 6.
Row 19 Rep row 7.
Row 20 K2, p2, k3, p5, k3, p2, sl last 2 sts to RH needle purlwise.
Row 21 Rep row 7.
Row 22 Rep row 10.
Row 23 Rep row 5.
Row 24 Rep row 12. Rep rows 1–24 6 times more.

STITCH KEY

☐	K on RS, P on WS
⊟	P on RS, K on WS
ⱽ	Sl st purlwise
⊐⊏	4-st RPC
⊏⊐	4-st LPC
⊐⊏⊏	7-st RPC
●	MB (bobble)

Cabled Brim
(19 sts)

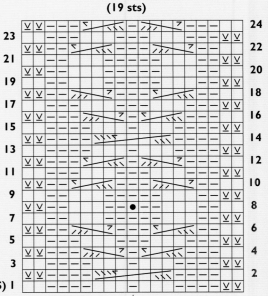

Jack Deutsch

34

Sew cast-on edge to bound-off edge forming a ring. Or, for provisional cast-on option, weave sts tog using Kitchener stitch.

Crown

With RS facing, B and circular needle, pick up and k 120 sts along one edge of cabled brim, beg and ending at seam (or joined sts). Place marker for end of rnd and sl marker every rnd. Work around in double moss st until piece measures 5"/12.5cm from beg (including cabled brim).

Crown shaping

Notes When dec, maintain double moss st by working either a k2tog or p2tog. Change to dpns (dividing sts evenly between three needles) when there are too few sts on circular needle.

Dec rnd 1 *Work double moss st over next 13 sts, work next 2 sts tog; rep from * around—112 sts. Work next rnd even.

Dec rnd 2 *Work double moss st over next 12 sts, work next 2 sts tog; rep from * around—104 sts. Work next rnd even.

Dec rnd 3 *Work double moss st over next 11 sts, work next 2 sts tog; rep from * around—96 sts. Work next rnd even.

Dec rnd 4 *Work double moss st over next 10 sts, work next 2 sts tog; rep from * around— 88 sts. Work next rnd even. Cont to work dec rnds as established, with one less st between decs, until 16 sts rem.

Next rnd [K2tog] 8 times—8 sts.

Next rnd [K2tog] 4 times—4 sts. Cut yarn leaving a 8"/20.5cm tail and thread through rem sts. Pull tog tightly and secure end.

YOU'LL NEED:

YARN (4)

1¾oz/50g or 50yd/45m of any worsted weight wool blend yarn in black (MC), lime green (A), turquoise (B), and red (C)

NEEDLES

one set (5) size 8 (5mm) double-pointed needles (dpns)
or size to obtain gauge
Size 8 (5mm) circular needle, 16"/40cm long

KNITTED MEASUREMENTS

Sized for 1 (2–4, 6) years
Circumference 17 (18, 19)"/43 (45.5, 48)cm
Length (with edge rolled) 6 (6, 7¼)"/15 (15, 18.5)cm

GAUGE

22 sts and 20 rnds to 4"/10cm over birdseye pat st using 2 colors and size 8 (5mm) needles.
Take time to check gauge.

STITCH GLOSSARY

Birdseye Pattern Stitch (even number of sts)
Rnds 1 and 3 *K1 with MC, k1 with A; rep from * around. **Rnds 2 and 4** *K1 with A, k1 with MC; rep from * around
Rnds 5 and 7 *K1 with MC, k1 with B; rep from * around. **Rnds 6 and 8** *K1 with B, k1 with MC; rep from * around

Rnds 9 and 11 *K1 with MC, k1 with C; rep from * around. **Rnds 10 and 12** *K1 with C, k1 with MC; rep from * around.
Rep these 12 rnds for birdseye pat st.

CAP

Beg at lower edge with circular needle and A, cast on 84 (90, 96) sts. Join to work in rnds. Pm to mark beg of rnd. Work in St st (k every rnd) for 9 rnds, inc 8 sts evenly across last rnd—92 (98, 104) sts. P next rnd. Beg with rnd 1, work in birdseye pat st for a total of 24 (24, 28) rnds and a total of 6 (6, 7) stripes.

Shape top

Note Cont to work birdseye pat st and stripe pat in next consecutive color.
Rnd 1 *Work 8 sts, [k2tog] twice; rep from * 6 (7, 7) times more, work 8 (2, 8) sts—78 (82, 88) sts. **Rnd 2** Work even in pat. **Rnd 3** *Work 6 sts, [k2tog] twice; rep from * 6 (7, 7) times more, work 8 (2, 8) sts—64 (66, 72) sts. **Rnd 4** Work even in pat. **Rnd 5** *Work 4 sts, [k2tog] twice; rep from * 6 (7, 7) times more, work 8 (2, 8) sts—50 (50, 56) sts. **Rnd 6** [K2tog] 25 (25, 28) times—25 (25, 28) sts. **Rnd 7** [K2tog] 12 (12, 14) times, k1 (1, 0)—13 (13, 14) sts. Cut yarn and pull through rem sts and draw up tightly to secure. Fasten off.

FINISHING

Block lightly, allowing lower edge to roll up without pressing.

HIS & HERS

Jack Deutsch

YOU'LL NEED:

YARN 🧶4

Pink hat 1¾oz/50g (1¾oz/50g, 2¾/75g) or 140yd/130m (140yd/130m, 210yd/200m) of any bulky weight wool blend yarn in pink (MC). 1¾oz/50g or 140yd/130m in gold (B) and yellow (C).

Blue hat 1¾oz/50g (1¾oz/50g, 2¾/75g) or 140yd/130m (140yd/130m, 210yd/200m) of any bulky weight wool blend yarn in light blue (MC). 1¾oz/50g or 140yd/130m in gold (B) and navy (C)

NEEDLES
Size 8 (5mm) circular knitting needle, 16"/41cm long
or size to obtain gauge
One set (4) size 8 (5mm) double-pointed needles (dpns)

ADDITIONAL MATERIALS
Stitch marker
Tapestry needle

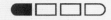

KNITTED MEASUREMENTS
Circumference 19 (21, 23)"/48.5 (53.5, 58.5) cm
Length 7½ (8, 8½)"/19 (20.5, 21.5)cm

GAUGE
22 sts and 22 rows to 4"/10cm over rib pattern using size 8 (5mm) needles.
Take time to check gauge.

STITCH GLOSSARY
Rib Pattern (multiple of 11 sts)
Rnd 1 *K4, [p1, k1] 3 times, p1; rep from * around.
Rep rnd 1 for rib pattern.

HAT
With MC cast on 88 (99, 110) sts. Join to work in rnds, taking care not to twist sts. Place marker for beg of rnds.
Next rnd Work 11-st rep of rib pat 8 (9, 10) times around.
Work in rib pat for 7 rnds more.
With A work 4 rnds rib pat.
With MC work 2 rnds rib pat.
With B work 2 rnds rib pat.
With MC work even until hat measures 6 (6½, 7)"/15 (16.5, 18)cm.

Shape crown
Next (dec) rnd *K4, p1, ssk, k1, k2tog, p1; rep from * around—72 (81, 90) sts.
Next rnd *K4, p1, k3, p1; rep from * around. Work even for 3 rnds.
Next (dec) rnd *Ssk, k2tog, p1, k3, p1; rep from * around—56 (63, 70) sts.
Next rnd *K2, p1, k3, p1; rep from * around. Work even for 3 rnds.
Next (dec) rnd *K2, p1, S2KP, p1; rep from * around—40 (45, 50) sts.
Next rnd *K2, p1, k1, p1; rep from * around.
Next (dec) rnd *K2tog, k1, ssk; rep from * around—24 (27, 30) sts.
Work 1 rnd even.

FINISHING
With yarn needle, pull yarn through rem sts several times, closing hole at top.

BABY Hats

YOU'LL NEED:

YARN (5)
1¾oz/50g or 55yd/50m of any bulky weight cotton blend yarn in purple, green, OR pink (MC)
1¾ oz/50g 50yd/45m of any bulky weight cotton blend yarn in white (A)
1¾oz/50g or 90yd/85m of any worsted weight "fun-fur" yarn in white (B)

NEEDLES
One set (4) size 9 (5.5mm) double-pointed needles (dpns)
or size to obtain gauge

ADDITIONAL MATERIALS
Stitch markers

KNITTED MEASUREMENTS
Sized for 0–3 (6, 12–18) months
Circumference 12½ (15, 17)"/32 (38, 43)cm
Length 6 (7, 8)"/15 (18, 20.5)cm

GAUGE
13 sts and 18 rows to 4"/10cm over St st with MC using size 9 (5.5mm) dpns.
Take time to check gauge.

STITCH GLOSSARY
Double Vertical Decrease (dv-dec)
Insert RH needle into the next 2 sts on LH needle one at a time as if to K. Sl them to the RH needle (sts are twisted). Return 2 sl sts to LH needle, keeping them twisted. Insert the RH needle through the back loops of the second and first sl sts and sl them together off the LH needle. P the next st. With the LH needle, pass the 2 sl sts over the p st and off the RH needle.

NOTE
Use 1 strand of A and B held tog for brim.

HAT
With A and B held tog, cast on 40 (48, 56) sts. Divide sts evenly over 3 needles. Pm for beg of rnd.
Rnd 1 Purl.
Rnd 2 Knit. Rep last 2 rnds twice more. P 1

rnd. Change to MC and work in St st until MC measures 2½ (3, 3½)"/6.5 (7.5, 10)cm
Shape crown
Next (dec) rnd *K7 (9, 11) sts, dv-dec; rep from * around—32 (40, 48) sts.
Work 1 rnd even.
Next (dec) rnd *K5 (7, 9), dv-dec; rep from * around—24 (32, 40) sts.
Work 1 rnd even.

Rep last 2 rnds, working 2 less k sts between dec's, 2 (3, 4) times more—8 sts. Cut yarn and pull through rem sts. Draw up tightly to secure. Fasten off.

HIGHLAND Helmet

YOU'LL NEED:

YARN ③
1¾oz/50g or 110yd/100m of any DK weight wool yarn in teal (A), evergreen (B), orange (C), brown (D), gold (E), coral (F), magenta (G), and light pink (H)

NEEDLES
One size 7 (4.5mm) circular needle, 16"/40cm long
or size to obtain gauge
One set (4) double-pointed needles (dpns) size 7 (4.5mm)
One pair size 7 (4.5mm) needles

ADDITIONAL MATERIALS
Size G/6 (4mm) crochet hook
10 stitch markers

■■■■▶

KNITTED MEASUREMENTS
Circumference before felting approx 24¾"/63cm
Circumference after felting approx 22"/55.5cm

GAUGE
19½ sts and 25 rows = 4"/10cm in St st over chart 1 using size 7 (4.5mm) circular needle (before felting).
Take time to check gauge.

NOTES
1 Hat is worked in rnds on circular needle until too small to fit on circular needle, then worked on dpns. Knit every rnd of hat.
2 Ear flaps are worked back and forth in rows of garter st.

HAT
With A and circular needle, cast on 120 sts. Join, taking care not to twist sts on needle. Place marker for beg of rnd, and sl marker every rnd.
Rnds 1–3 With A, knit.
Rnds 4 and 5 *K2 A, k2 H; rep from * around.
Rnds 6 and 7 With A, knit.
Rnd 8 *K2 G, k2 A; rep from * around.
Rnd 9 With C, knit.
Rnd 10 With E, knit.
Rnds 11 and 12 With A, knit.
Rnd 13 With F, knit.
Beg chart 1
Rnds 14–27 Work chart 1, working 12-st rep 10 times.
Rnd 28 With E, knit.
Rnd 29 With G, knit.
Rnd 30 With B, knit.
Rnd 31 With C, knit.
Dec rnd 32 With C, k5, *k2tog, k10; rep from *, end last rep k5—110 sts.
Rnd 33 *K5 A, k5 F; rep from * around.
Dec rnd 34 With C, k 1 rnd, dec 2 sts evenly—108 sts.
Beg chart 2
Rnds 35–40 Work chart 2, working 6-st rep 18 times.
Dec rnd 41 *K1 A, k1 H; rep from *, AT SAME TIME, work decs as foll: k3, *ssk, k2, k2tog, k6; rep from *, end last rep k3—90 sts.
Rnd 42 With D, knit.
Dec rnd 43 With E, k2, *ssk, k2, k2tog, k4; rep from *, end k2—72 sts.
Rnd 44 With D, knit.
Dec rnd 45 With E, k1, *ssk, k2, k2tog, k2; rep from *, end k1—54 sts.
Dec rnd 46 With E, *ssk, k2, k2tog; rep from * around—36 sts.
Rnd 47 With A, knit.
Dec rnd 48 With A, *ssk, k2tog; rep from * around—18 sts.
Rnd 49 With A, knit.
Dec rnd 50 With A, *k2tog; rep from * around—9 sts.
Cut yarn leaving 6"/15.5cm tail and thread through rem 9 sts. Pull tight and secure end.

Ear flaps
With hat upside down, RS and center back facing, and A, beg in 19th st to the left of center back, pick up and k 21 sts.
Rows 1–5 With A, knit.
Rows 6–9 With B, knit.
Rows 10 and 11 With D, knit.
Rows 12 and 13 With E, knit.
Rows 14–17 With A, knit.
Dec row 18 With B, k2, ssk, k to last 4 sts, k2tog, k2—19 sts.
Row 19 With B, knit.
Rows 20–23 Rep row 18 and 19 twice—15 sts.
Rows 24 and 25 With G, rep rows 18 and 19—13 sts.
Rows 26–31 With A, rep rows 18 and 19 three times—7 sts.
Dec row 32 With A, k2, sl 1, k2tog, psso, k2—5 sts. Bind off.
Work 2nd ear flap to correspond to first one.

FINISHING
With RS facing and crochet hook, beg at center back lower edge of hat, work sc evenly around lower edge, alternating 1 st A, 1 st D.

Felting
Set washer for hot wash, longest cycle and lowest water level. Add small amount of mild detergent. Do not use your washer's spin cycle. While agitating, check on the progress every 5 minutes. Set washer back to agitate longer if needed. When the hat is felted to the approx circumference, remove and rinse by hand in cool water. Roll in a towel to remove as much water as possible.

Chart 1

14

5

3

1

12-st rep

Chart 2

6

1

6-st rep

Color Key

■ Teal (A)

■ Evergreen (B)

■ Brown (D)

■ Gold (E)

□ Coral (F)

■ Magenta (G)

□ Light Pink (H)

RIBBED Cap

Eye[4]Media

YOU'LL NEED:

YARN
1¾oz/50g or 110yd/100m of any worsted weight self-striping wool yarn

NEEDLES
One pair size 8 (5mm) straight needles *or size to obtain gauge*
1 set (4) size 8 (5mm) double-pointed needles (dpns)
or size to obtain gauge

KNITTED MEASUREMENTS
Circumference (slightly stretched) 21"/53cm
Length 7"/18cm

GAUGE
20 sts and 28 rows/rnds to 4"/10cm over k4, p4 rib using size 8 (5mm) straight needles OR dpns.
Take time to check gauge.

NOTE
Cap can be worked either flat or in the round.

STITCH GLOSSARY
Straight Needles
K4, P4 Rib Pattern
Row 1 (RS) K2, *p4, k4; rep from *, end last rep k2 instead of k4.
Row 2 K the knit and p the purl sts.
Rep row 2 for k4, p4 rib pat.

Double Pointed Needles
K4, P4 Rib Pattern
Rnd 1 *K4, p4; rep from * around.
Rep rnd 1 for k4, p4 rib pat.

CAP
Straight Knitting
With straight needles, cast on 106 sts.
Row 1 (RS) K1 (selvage st), work in k4, p4 rib pat to last st, k1 (selvage st). Work in k4, p4 rib pat as established (with k1 selvage st each side of row) until piece measures 6"/15cm from beg, end with a WS row.
Shape top
Row 1 (RS) K3, *p1, p2tog, p1, k1, k2tog, k1; rep from * to last 3 sts, end k3—81 sts.
Row 2 K the knit and p the purl sts.
Row 3 K3, *p2tog, p1, k2tog, k1; rep from * to last 3 sts, k3—56 sts.
Row 4 K the knit and p the purl sts.
Row 5 K3, *p2tog, k2; rep from * to last 3 sts, k3—43 sts.
Row 6 K the knit and p the purl sts.
Row 7 K1, *k2tog, p1; rep from * to last 3 sts, k2tog, k1—29 sts.
Row 8 K1, *p1, p2tog; rep from *, end k1—20 sts.
Row 9 [K2tog] 10 times—10 sts*. Cut yarn leaving a long end for sewing back seam. Pull through rem 10 sts and draw up tightly to secure. Sew back seam.

FINISHING
Do not block or flatten rib.

Circular Knitting
With dpn, cast on 104 sts and divide sts on 3 needles with 34 sts on needle 1, 36 sts on needle 2 and 34 sts on needle 3. Join, being careful not to twist sts and pm to mark beg of rnd. Work in k4, p4 rib pat in rnds for 6"/15cm
Shape top
Rnd 1 *K1, k2tog, k1, p1, p2tog, p1; rep from * around—78 sts.
Rnd 2 K the knit sts and p the purl sts.
Rnd 3 *K2tog, k1, p2tog, p1; rep from * around—52 sts.
Rnd 4 K the knit and p the purl sts.
Rnd 5 *K2, p2tog; rep from * around—39 sts.
Rnd 6 K the knit and p the purl sts.
Rnd 7 *K2tog, p1; rep from * around—26 sts.
Rnd 8 K2, *k2tog, k1; rep from * around—18 sts.
Rnd 9 [K2tog] 9 times—9 sts. Cut yarn leaving an end for sewing top. Pull through rem 9 sts and draw up tightly to secure. Fasten off.

FINISHING
Do not block or flatten rib.

AVIATOR Cap

Jack Deutsch

YOU'LL NEED:

YARN (6)
7oz/200g of any super-bulky weight wool yarn

NEEDLES
Size 8 (5mm) circular needle, 16"/41cm long *or size to obtain gauge*
One set (4) size 8 (5mm) double-pointed needles (dpns) *or size to obtain gauge*
Size 7 (4.5mm) needles

ADDITIONAL MATERIALS
Stitch markers

KNITTED MEASUREMENTS
Circumference 21"/53.5cm
Length 9½"/24cm

STITCH GLOSSARY
Seed St (worked over an even number of sts)
Rnd 1 *P1, k1; rep from * to end.
Rnd 2 Knit the purl sts and purl the knit sts.
Rep rnd 2 for seed st.

GAUGE
15 sts and 20 rows to 4"/10cm over seed st using size 8 (5mm) needles.
Each 13-st section measures 3½"/9cm.
Take time to check gauge.

HAT
With larger circular needle, cast on 78 sts. Join to work in rnds, taking care not to twist sts. Place marker for end of rnd.
Rnd 1 *K2, [p1, k1] 5 times, k1, place marker; rep from * around—6 sections.
Rnd 2 *K1, [p1, k1] 6 times; rep from * around.
Rep rnds 1 and 2 until hat measures 7"/18cm from beg, end with rnd 2.

Shape crown
Next (dec) rnd *Ssk, work in

established seed st to 2 sts before marker, k2tog; rep from * around—66 sts.
Next rnd *K2, work in seed st to marker; rep from * around.
Rep last 2 rnds 4 more times—18 sts.
Next rnd *S2KP; rep from * around—6 sts.
Cut yarn, draw through rem sts twice and pull tightly.

Earflaps
Mark 1 section as center back. With smaller needles and RS facing, work in section to left of center back, pick up and knit 10 sts in purl bumps behind cast-on row.
Slipping first st of every row, knit 11 rows.

Shape ends
Next (dec) row (RS) Sl 1, ssk, k to last 3 sts, k2tog, k1—9 sts.
Next row Sl 1, knit to end of row.
Rep last 2 rows until 5 sts rem.
Next row Sl 1, k3tog, k1—3 sts.

I-cord ties
Work 3 rem sts in I-cord until tie measures

6"/15cm. K3tog, fasten off last st. Weave end into cord.
Work second earflap in section on other side center back.

Brim
Mark the center of each of the 3 remaining front sections. With RS facing and smaller needles, beg at first marker, pick up and knit 5 sts in first section, 10 sts in middle section, and 5 sts in third section, end at last marker—20 sts.
Slipping first st of every row, knit 5 rows.

Shape brim
Next (dec) row Ssk, knit to last 2 sts, k2tog—18 sts.
Rep dec row twice—14 sts.
Bind off knitwise on WS.

STRIPED Hat

Rose Callahan

KNITTED MEASUREMENTS
Circumference (around ribbed brim)
17"/43cm
Length 11"/28cm

GAUGE
25 sts and 36 rnds to 4"/10cm over St st using size 6 (4mm) needles.
Take time to check gauge.

HAT
With size 6 (4mm) circular needle and A, cast on 108 sts, place marker (pm) and join, being careful not to twist. Work in k2, p2 rib until piece measures 2"/5cm from beg. Cont with A, work in St st (k every rnd) until piece measures 4¼"/11cm from beg. Cont in St st, with B work for 2½"/6.5cm. With A, work for 2½"/6.5cm. With B work until piece measures 9¾"/24.5cm from beg.

YOU'LL NEED:
YARN ❸
2oz/55g or 200yd/190m of any DK weight wool yarn in both pink (A) and green (B)

NEEDLES
Size 6 (4mm) circular needle, 16"/40cm long *or size to obtain gauge*
One set (5) size 6 (4mm) double-pointed needles (dpns)

ADDITIONAL MATERIALS
Stitch marker
Tapestry needle

Shape crown
Note Change to dpns when sts no longer comfortably fit on circular needle.
Cont in St st with B and beg to shape crown as foll:
Next (dec) rnd *K7, k2tog; rep from * to end—96 sts. Knit 1 rnd.
Next (dec) rnd *K6, k2tog; rep from * around—84 sts. Knit 1 rnd.
Next (dec) rnd *K5, k2tog, rep from * around—72 sts. Knit 1 rnd.
Next (dec) rnd *K4, k2tog, rep from * around—60 sts. Cont to dec every rnd working 1 less st before each k2tog until 24 sts rem.
Next (dec) rnd *K2tog; rep from * around—12 sts. Cut yarn leaving long tail and thread through rem sts.

FINISHING
With tapestry needle and 36"/91.5cm length of A, beg on WS just above rib, sew running st up one column of sts to crown, turn and sew running st down next column of sts, to beg of rib. Pull tails to gather to desired shape. Tie off.

RIB BAND Hat

Eye[4]Media

KNITTED MEASUREMENTS
Circumference 21"/53cm
Length 8½"/21.5cm

GAUGE
17 sts and 22 rows to 4"/10cm over k3, p2 rib (slightly stretched) using 2 strands of yarn and size 7 (4.5mm) needles.
Take time to check gauge.

NOTE
Work with 2 strands of yarn held together throughout.

CAP
Beg at lower edge with 2 strands of yarn and size 7 (4.5mm) needles, cast on 92 sts.
Row 1 (RS) K1 (selvage st), *k3, p2; rep from *, end k1 (selvage st).
Row 2 K1, *k2, p3; rep from *, end k1.
Rep these 2 rows for k3, p2 rib until piece measures 7½"/19cm from beg.
Shape top
Row 1 (RS) K1, *k2tog, k1, p2; rep from *, end k1 —74 sts.

Row 2 Work in k2, p2 rib as established.
Row 3 K1, *k2tog, p2; rep from *, end k1 —56 sts.
Row 4 K1, *k2, p1; rep from *, end k1.
Row 5 K1, *k1, p2tog; rep from *, end k1 —38 sts.
Row 6 Work in k1, p1 rib as established.
Row 7 K1, [k2tog] 18 times, k1 —20 sts.
Row 8 Purl. Cut yarn, leaving long end for sewing. Pull through rem sts on needle and draw up tightly and secure. Fasten off but leave end for seaming with band later.

BAND
With 2 strands of yarn and size 7 (4.5mm) needles, cast on 20 sts.
Row 1 (RS) Knit.
Rows 2, 4, 6 and 8 Purl.
Row 3 K1, *sl next 3 sts to cn and hold to back, k3, k3 from cn, k3; rep from * once more, k1.
Row 5 Knit.
Row 7 K1, *k3, sl next 3 sts to cn and hold to front, k3, k3 from cn; rep from * once more, k1.
Rep rows 1–8 for 21"/53cm. Bind off.

FINISHING
Block lightly to measurements. Pin cable band to lower edge of hat at ½"/1.5cm from lower edge. Sew back seam along with band in place.

CAT Hat

KNITTED MEASUREMENTS
Sized for 6 (12, 24) months
Circumference 15 (17, 18½)"/38 (43, 47)cm
Length (with edge rolled) 5½ (5¾, 6)"/14 (14.5, 15)cm

GAUGE
19 sts and 28 rows/rnds to 4"/10cm over St st using size 6 (4mm) needles.
Take time to check gauge.

STITCH GLOSSARY
Large bobble With color B, k into front, back, front and back of 1 st (for 4 sts in 1 st), turn. P4, turn. K4, turn. P4, turn. K2tog twice, turn. P2tog, then sl resulting st back to RH needle.
Small bobble With color B, k into front and back of 1 st (for 2 sts), turn. P2, turn. K2, turn. P2tog, then sl resulting st back to RH needle.

HAT
Note If desired, entire hat may be worked using dpn. Or work with a circular needle until there are too few sts to work comfortably, then change to dpns.
With A and circular needle, cast on 72 (80, 88) sts. Join being careful not to twist sts.

Pm to mark beg of rnd. Work in St st (k every rnd) for 2"/5cm.
Next rnd With A, k5 (6, 7), with B make large bobble, k with A until 6 (7, 8) sts from end of rnd, with B make large bobble, k with A to end of rnd.
Next rnd With A, k3 (4, 5), with B make small bobble, k3 with A, with B make small bobble, k with A until 8 (9, 10) sts from end of rnd, with B make small bobble, k3 with A, with B make small bobble, k with A to end of rnd.
Next rnd Work even with A.
Next rnd With A, k4 (5, 6), with B make small bobble, k1 with A, with B make small bobble, k with A until 7 (8, 9) sts from end of rnd, with B make small bobble, k1 with A, with B make small bobble, k with A to end of rnd.
Then cont to k every rnd with A only until piece measures 4¾ (5, 5¼)"/12 (12.5, 13.5)cm from beg, with edge unrolled. Change to B and k1 rnd.

Crown shaping
Note When there are too few sts to fit circular needle, change to dpns.
Dec rnd *K6, skp; rep from * to end—63 (70, 77) sts. K 1 rnd.
Dec rnd *K5, skp; rep from * to end—54 (60, 66) sts. K 1 rnd.
Dec rnd *K4, skp; rep from * to end—45 (50, 55) sts. K 1 rnd.
Cont to work dec rnds every other rnd in this way 3 times more, having 1 st less before dec every dec rnd and 18 (20, 22) sts rem. Change to C.
Next rnd [skp] 9 (10, 11) times—9 (10, 11) sts. K1 rnd with C.
Next rnd [skp] 4 (5, 5) times, k1 (0, 1)—5 (5, 6) sts.
Draw yarn through rem sts on needles, pull up tightly and fasten off.

Tail
Note Work back and forth in rows on 2 dpns. With A, cast on 8 sts. Work in St st (k 1 row, p 1 row) for 4½"/11.5cm. Change to B and cont for 1½"/4cm more. Bind off. Sew sides of rows tog to form tail, sewing the B section closed. Locate center back of hat (bobbles form the paws at center front) and sew end of tail to center back.
Ears (make 2)
With B, cast on 7 sts. Working back and forth in rows with 2 dpn, work 4 rows in St st.
Next row (RS) K1, skp, k1, k2tog, k1—5 sts. P 1 row.
Next row Skp, k1, k2tog—3 sts. Draw yarn through rem sts and pull up lightly. Sew open ends of ears to hat, skipping one decreased wedge for top of head and sewing ears along 2 wedges at each side.

FINISHING
Using photo as a guide, embroider eyes, mouth and whiskers using D and straight sts.

Quenet

SCOTTY Cap

YOU'LL NEED:

YARN 4

3½oz/100g or 170yd/150m of any worsted weight wool yarn in grey (MC) and 1¾oz/50g or 85yd/75m of any worsted weight "fun-fur" yarn in black (A)

NEEDLES

One set (5) size 7 (4.5mm) double-pointed needles (dpns)
or size to obtain gauge

ADDITIONAL MATERIALS

1yd/1m .5mm wide red ribbon

KNITTED MEASUREMENTS

Sized for Child (Adult Woman)
Circumference 17 (19)"/43 (48)cm
Length (with lower edge rolled) 7¼ (8½)"/18.5 (21.5)cm

GAUGE

19 sts and 26 rows to 4"/10cm over St st using MC and size 7 (4.5mm) dpns.
Take time to check gauge.

NOTES

1 Use double strand A when working chart.
2 When changing colors foll chart, twist new yarn around working yarn to avoid holes in work.

HAT

Beg at lower edge with MC, cast on 81 (90) sts. Divide sts on 4 needles with 20 sts on first 3 needles and 21 sts on needle 4 for Child's size; 22 sts on needles 1 and 3 and 23 sts on needles 2 and 4 for Woman's size. Join, being careful not to twist sts and pm to mark beg of rnd. K10 rnds, p4 rnds for double rolled edge. Then cont in St st, k5 rnds.

Beg chart pat

Rnd 1 (RS) *With MC, k5 (3), work 15 sts (with double strand A) of chart pat; rep from * 3 (4) times more, end k1 (0) MC. Cont to foll chart in this way through rnd 15. Then cont in St st with MC only for 1¾ (3)"/4.5 (7.5)cm.

Shape crown

Rnd 1 *K7 (8), k2tog; rep from * 8 times more—72 (81) sts.
Rnd 2 Knit.
Rnd 3 *K6 (7), k2tog; rep from * 8 times more—63 (72) sts.
Rnd 4 Knit.
Rnd 5 *K5 (6), k2tog; rep from * 8 times more—54 (63) sts.
Rnd 6 Knit.
Rnd 7 *K4 (5), k2tog; rep from * 8 times more—45 (54) sts.
Rnd 8 Knit.
Rnd 9 *K3 (4), k2tog; rep from * 8 times more—36 (45) sts.
Rnd 10 Knit.
For Child's size only
Rnd 11 [K2tog] 18 times—18 sts.
Rnd 12 [K3tog] 6 times—6 sts.
For Woman's size only
Rnd 11 *K3, k2tog; rep from * 8 times more—36 sts.
Rnd 12 Knit.
Rnd 13 [K2tog] 18 times—18 sts.
Rnd 14 [K3tog] 6 times—6 sts.
Both sizes
Change to double strand A and work rem 6 sts even for 1"/2.5cm.
Next rnd [K2tog] 3 times. K3tog and fasten off.

FINISHING

Block lightly being sure to keep lower edge rolled. Cut 4 (5) 7"/18cm lengths of ribbon and tie around the neck of each Scottie dog around. Tie ribbon in bows as shown.

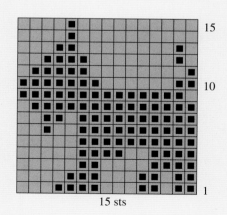

15 sts

Color Key

Grey (MC)

Black (A), double strand

FUZZY Helmet

YOU'LL NEED:

YARN ⓸
3½oz/100g or 180yd/170m of any
worsted weight "fun fur" yarn

NEEDLES
One set (4) size 10 (6mm) double-
pointed needles (dpns)
or size to obtain gauge
Size 10 (6mm) circular needle
18"/46cm long

ADDITIONAL MATERIALS
Size L (8mm) crochet hook
Stitch marker

KNITTED MEASUREMENTS
Circumference 19"/48cm
Length 7"/17.5cm

GAUGE
14 sts and 24 rows to 4"/10cm over seed st
using size 10 (6mm) needles.
Take time to check gauge.

STITCH GLOSSARY
Seed Stitch
Row 1 *K1, p1; rep from * to end.
Row 2 K the purl sts and p the knit sts.
Rep row 2 for seed st.
Inc 1 K into front and back of st.

CAP
With crochet hook, ch 50 to make one tie.
Sl st to one dpn and work first earflap on
dpn as foll:
Row 1 Inc 1—2 sts.

Row 2 K1, inc 1—3 sts.
Row 3 K1, p1, inc 1—4 sts.
Row 4 P1, k1, p1 inc 1—5 sts.
Rows 5 and 6 Beg with a p1, work in seed st.
Row 7 *P1, k1; rep from * to last st, inc 1—6 sts.
Row 8 *K1, p1; rep from * to last st, inc
1—7 sts.
Rows 9 and 10 Beg with k1, work in seed st.
Row 11 *K1, p1; rep from * to last st, inc
1—8 sts.
Row 12 *P1, k1; rep from * to last st, inc
1—9 sts.
Rep rows 7–12 once—13 sts.
Rep rows 7–10 once—15 sts.
Cut yarn and leave sts on needle.
Make a second earflap in same way, but
transfer this earflap to circular needle and
cast on 24 sts for front of hat, work rem
earflap onto needle, working in seed st,
cast on 13 sts for back, pm.

Crown
Join and cont in seed st on 67 sts for
32 rnds (approx 4"/10cm). P 5 rnds, k 5

rnds, dec 1 st at end of last rnd—66 sts.
Divide sts evenly over 3 dpn (22 sts on
each needle).

TOP SHAPING
Dec Rnd 1 *K9, k2tog; rep from *
around—60 sts. K 1 rnd.
Dec Rnd 2 *K8, k2tog; rep from *
around—54 sts. K 1 rnd.
Cont in this way to dec 6 sts every other
rnd until 2 sts rem on each needle.
Work 6 rnds even for tip. Cut yarn and pull
through sts.

FINISHING
With tapestry needle and yarn, pass a running st around crown to form tuck. Make
two 2"/5cm pom-poms and attach to end
of ties.

GOING Loopy

Quenet

YOU'LL NEED:

YARN 5
5¼oz/150g or 150yd/140m of any bulky weight variegated wool blend yarn

NEEDLES
One pair size 13 (9mm) needles
or size to obtain gauge

KNITTED MEASUREMENTS
Circumference 19"/48cm
Length 8 ½"/21.5cm

GAUGE
10 sts and 21 rows to 4"/10cm over garter st using size 13 (9mm) needles.
Take time to check gauge.

STITCH GLOSSARY
Stitch Pattern
Row 1 (WS) K19, p1, k to end.
Row 2 K6, sl 1, k to 2 sts from end, w&t.
Row 3 and all WS rows K to 7 sts from end, p1, k to end.
Row 4 K6, sl 1, k to 4 sts from end, w&t.
Row 6 K6, sl 1, k to 6 sts from end, w&t.
Row 8 K6, sl 1, k to 8 sts from end, w&t.
Row 10 K6, sl 1, k to 6 sts from end, w&t.
Row 12 K6, sl 1, k to 4 sts from end, w&t.
Row 14 K6, sl 1, k to 2 sts from end, w&t.
Row 16 K6, sl 1, k to end.
Rep these 16 rows for stitch pat.

Short Row Wrapping (wrap and turn—w&t)
1 Wyib, sl next st purlwise.
2 Move yarn between the needles to the front.
3 Sl the same st back to LH needle. Turn work, bring yarn to the p side between needles. One st is wrapped. When short rows are completed, work to just before wrapped st, insert RH needle under the wrap and knitwise into the wrapped st, k them tog.

CAP
With waste yarn and using provisional cast on (see page 16), cast on 26 sts. Change to working yarn. Work 16 rows of st pat 6 times. Work row 1 once more. Cut yarn, leaving 30"/76cm tail for grafting.

FINISHING
Drop last 2 sts off needle and let them hang. Undo waste yarn holding first row of knitting. Using Kitchener stitch, graft last row of knitting to first row.

Sew gap at top of hat closed.
Brim
Unravel all rows of dropped sts and tie each loop with an overhand knot close to knitting to finish fringe. Fold brim at sl st row.

ELEGANT Earflap Hat

YOU'LL NEED:

YARN
3½oz/100g or 220yd/200m of any
worsted weight wool yarn.

NEEDLES
One size 7 (4.5mm) circular needle
16"/40cm long
or size to obtain gauge
One set (5) size 7 (4.5mm) double-
pointed needles (dpns)

ADDITIONAL MATERIALS
Stitch markers

KNITTED MEASUREMENTS
Circumference 22"/56cm
Width of earflap 14"/35.5cm
Length 10"/25.5cm

GAUGE
18 sts and 23 rows to 4"/10cm over chart
pat using size 7 (4.5mm) needles.
Take time to check gauge.

NOTE
Hat is worked from the lower edge up. The
earflap is worked back and forth in rows
and additional stitches are cast on for the
crown to complete the hat in the round.

EARFLAP
With circular needle, cast on 67 sts. Do not
join.
Next row (WS) K3, p to last 3 sts, k3.
Beg chart
Next row (RS) K3, work 10-st rep of row 1
six times across, work last st of chart, k3.
Cont to work chart in this manner through
row 8. Rep rows 1–8 three times more,
then rep rows 1 and 2 once. Piece measures approx 6"/15cm from beg.

Crown
Next (joining) row (RS) K3, work chart row,
work last st of chart, k3, cast on 33 sts, pm
for beg of rnd—100 sts.
Join and beg working in the round
as foll:
Next rnd P3, cont chart pat over 61 sts, p
to end.
Next rnd K3, cont chart pat over 61 sts, k to
end.
Cont in this manner until 5 rnds have been
worked over cast-on sts and rnd 8 of chart
is complete.
Next rnd K3, work chart rnd 1 to end of rnd,
remove marker, complete last 10-st chart
rep over next 3 sts, pm for new beg of rnd.
Work in chart pat until rnd 8 of chart has
been completed twice more.

Shape crown
Note Change to double-pointed needles
when there are too few sts to fit comfort-
ably on circular needle.
Rnd 1 (dec) [SKP, k2, yo, S2KP, yo, k3] 10
times—90 sts. **Rnd 2** Knit.
Rnd 3 (dec) [SKP, k1, yo, S2KP, yo, k3] 10
times—80 sts. **Rnd 4** Knit.
Rnd 5 (dec) [SKP, yo, S2KP, yo, k3] 10
times—70 sts.
Rnds 6, 8, 10, 12 K to last st, pm for new
beg of rnd.
Rnd 7(dec) Remove old marker, [SKP, yo,
SK2P, yo, k2] 10 times—60 sts
Rnd 9 (dec) Remove old marker, [SKP, yo,
SK2P, yo, k1] 10 times—50 sts
Rnd 11 (dec) Remove old marker, [SKP, yo,
SK2P, yo] 10 times—40 sts.
Rnd 13 (dec) Remove old marker, [k1, SK2P]
10 times—20 sts.
Rnd 14 (dec) Remove old marker, [k2tog]
10 times—10 sts
Cut yarn leaving a long tail and draw
through rem sts.

FINISHING
Make two 2"/5cm pompoms and attach to
ends of earflaps (see photo).

CHART

```
                          8
-  -  -  -  O ⋏ O -  -  -  7
-  -  -  O  ⋏  O -  -  -  5
-  -  O  ⋏  O  -  -  3
-  O  ⋏  O  -  1
```
└─── 10-st rep ───┘

STITCH KEY

☐ k on RS, p on WS   ⊙ yo

⊟ p on RS, k on WS   ⋏ S2KP

PRETTY in Pink

Eye[4]Media

KNITTED MEASUREMENTS
Circumference 21"/53cm
Length 8¼"/21cm

GAUGE
16 sts and 20 rows to 4"/10cm over St st using 2 strands of yarn and size 10½ (7mm) needles.
Take time to check gauge.

STITCH GLOSSARY
Horseshoe Cable Pattern
(multiple of 16 sts and worked in rnds)
Rnds 1, 2 and 3 *K12, p4; rep from * around.
Rnd 4 *Sl 3 sts to cn and hold to back, k3, k3 from cn, sl next 3 sts to cn and hold to front, k3, k3 from cn, p4; rep from * around.
Rep rnds 1–4 for horseshoe cable pat.
Note Work with 2 strands of yarn held together throughout.

CAP
Beg at lower edge with circular needle and 2 strands of yarn, cast on 96 sts. Join to work in rnds. Pm at beg of rnd. Work in k1, p1 rib for 2"/5cm. Then work in horseshoe cable pat for 3"/7.5cm.
Dec rnd *Work 12 sts, p1, p2tog, p1; rep from * around—90 sts. Work even for 3 rnds.
Dec rnd *Work 12 sts, p1, p2tog; rep from * around—84 sts. Work even for 3 rnds.
Dec rnd *Work 12 sts, p2tog; rep from * around—78 sts. Change to dpns to accommodate fewer sts.
Next rnd *[K2tog] 6 times, p1; rep from * around—42 sts.
Next rnd *[K2tog] 3 times, p1; rep from * around—24 sts.
Next rnd *K2tog, sl 1, p1, psso; rep from * around—12 sts. Cut yarn leaving a 12"/30.5 length. Pull yarn through rem sts and draw up tightly to secure.

FINISHING
I-cord
With 2 dpns, cast on 3 sts. *K3, do not turn. Slide sts to beg of needle and bring yarn around from back to k3 from same position again. Rep from * for I-cord for 6"/15cm. Bind off.

Tassel
Wind yarn 42 times around a 4½"/11.5cm cardboard. Pull strand of yarn through lps at top and tie tightly to fasten. Cut other end of yarn at opposite side of cardboard. Wind yarn around top of tassel at 1"/2.5cm from top. Fasten to end of I-cord. Fasten other end of I-cord to top of cap.

HERRINGBONE Cloche

Eye[4]Media

YOU'LL NEED:

YARN (3)
3½oz/100g or 230yd/200m of any DK weight wool yarn

NEEDLES
One pair size 6 (4mm) needles
or size to obtain gauge
One pair size 7 (4.5mm) needles for casting on only
Size 6 (4mm) circular needle 20"/50cm long

ADDITIONAL MATERIALS
1 yd/1m of leather cord

KNITTED MEASUREMENTS
Circumference 20"/51cm
Length (excluding brim) 6"/15cm

GAUGE
30 sts and 26 rows to 4"/10cm over herringbone pat st using size 6 (4mm) needles.
Take time to check gauge.

STITCH GLOSSARY
Herringbone Pattern Stitch
(over an odd number of sts)
Row 1 (WS) *P2tog and leave sts on LH needle, purl first st again, drop both sts tog from LH needle; rep from *, end p1.
Row 2 (RS) *Sl 1 wyib, k1, with LH needle raise up sl st slightly, pull RH needle through raised st like a psso but do not drop raised st from LH needle, k into back lp of raised st and drop from needle; rep from *, end k1.
Rep rows 1 and 2 for herringbone pat st.

HAT
Side Crown Section (make 2)
With size 7 (4.5mm) needles, cast on 55 sts. Change to size 6 (4mm) needles and work in herringbone pat st for 4 rows.
**Dec row 1 (WS) P2tog (for dec 1 st); rep from * of row 1 of pat, end p1.
Dec row 2 (RS) k2tog (for dec 1 st); rep from * of row 2 to last 2 sts, k2tog (for dec 1 st).

Dec row 3 (WS) Rep from * of row 1 to last 2 sts, p2tog (for dec 1 st)—4 sts dec'd for 51 sts. Work even for 1 row **. Rep between **'s 3 times more—39 sts.
+Dec row 4 (WS) [P2tog] twice; rep from * of row 1 to end.
Dec row 5 (RS) [K2tog] twice; rep from * of row 2 to end +.
Rep between +'s 5 times more—15 sts.
Dec row 6 [P2tog] twice, rep from * of row 1 to last 5 sts, [p2tog] twice, p1.
Dec row 7 [K2tog] twice, rep from * of row 2 to last 5 sts, [k2tog] twice, k1.
Next row [P2tog] 3 times, p1.
Next row SK2P, k1, turn. Bind off 1 st and fasten off.
Center Crown Section (make 1)
With size 7 (4.5mm) needles, cast on 59 sts. Change to size 6 (4mm) needles and work in herringbone pat st for 4 rows. Then cont as for side crown section, beg at ** and working up to Dec row 4—43 sts. Rep between +'s a total of 5 times—23 sts. Then rep dec rows 6 and 7 twice—7 sts.
Next row (WS) [P2tog] 3 times, p1.
Next row SK2P, k1, turn. Bind off 1 st and fasten off.
Sew the 2 side crown sections to center crown section leaving back seam open.

BRIM
With RS facing and size 6 (4mm) circular needle, pick up and k 175 sts evenly around lower edge of joined crown pieces.
Row 1 (WS) Work row 1 of herringbone pat st.
Row 2 (RS) Work 10 sts, yo, work 34 sts, yo, [work 44 sts, yo] twice, work 34 sts, yo, work 9 sts.
Row 3 (WS) Work row 1 of pat st, working a p2tog into yo of previous row plus the next st, then pick up 1 st in row below and lift to LH needle to make next p2tog—185 sts. The 5 yo's of previous row will become 10 extra sts or 2 sts will be added for each yo in this way.
Row 4 Work 6 sts, yo, work 44 sts, yo, work 38 sts, yo, work 46 sts, yo, work 44 sts, yo,

work 7 sts.
Row 5 Rep row 3—195 sts. Cont to inc in this way, adding 5 yo's every RS row (not directly over yo's of previous inc row) and a total of 10 sts every WS row 8 times more, AT THE SAME TIME, shape back brim with short rows beg on row 8 as foll:
Short row 8 Working 5 spaced yo's as before, work to last 7 sts, w&t.
Short row 9 Working 10 incs as before, work to last 7 sts, w&t.
Short row 10 Working 5 spaced yo's work to last 13 sts, w&t.
Short row 11 Working 10 incs as before, work to last 13 sts, w&t.
Short row 12 Working 5 spaced yo's, work to last 19 sts, w&t.
Short row 13 Working 10 incs as before, work to last 19 sts, w&t.
Short row 14 Working 5 spaced yo's, work to last 25 sts, w&t.
Short row 15 Working 10 incs as before, work to last 25 sts, w&t.
Row 16 Working 5 spaced yo's, work across all sts to end, working into wrapped sts to close up holes.
Row 17 Working 10 incs as before, work all sts to end, working into wrapped sts to close up holes.
Next row (RS) Bind off sts as foll: *p1, p2tog; bind off 1 st; rep from * across.

FINISHING
Block brim flat very carefully. Do not block rest of hat. Sew back brim seam. Draw leather cord through hat at brim pick-up line.

TRAVELING Cables

Jack Deutch

YOU'LL NEED:

YARN ④
3½oz/100g or 180yd/160m of any worsted weight wool yarn

NEEDLES
Size 9 (5.5mm) circular needle, 16"/40.5cm long
or size to obtain gauge
One set (4) size 9 (5.5mm) double-pointed needles (dpns)

ADDITIONAL MATERIALS
Cable needle (cn)
Stitch marker

KNITTED MEASUREMENTS
Circumference 18"/45.5cm

GAUGE
18 sts and 24 rnds to 4"/10cm over St st using size 9 (5.5mm) circular needle.
Take time to check gauge.

STITCH GLOSSARY
8-st RPC Sl next 5 sts to cn and hold in *back*, k3, (k3, p2) from cn.
6-st RC Sl next 3 sts to cn and hold in *back*, k3, k3 from cn.

HAT
With circular needle, cast on 96 sts. Join taking care not to twist sts on needle. Place marker for end of rnd and sl marker every rnd.
Rnds 1–5 *P6, k6; rep from * around.
Rnd 6 *P4, 8-st RPC; rep from * around.
Rnds 7–15 *P4, k6, p2; rep from * around.
Rnd 16 *P2, 8-st RPC, p2; rep from * around.
Rnds 17–25 *P2, k6, p4; rep from * around.
Rnd 26 *8-st RPC, p4; rep from * around.
Crown shaping
Note Change to dpns (dividing sts evenly between three needles) when there are too few sts on circular needle.
Rnd (dec) 27 *K6, p2tog, p4; rep from * around—88 sts.
Rnds 28–33 *K6, p5; rep from * around.
Rnd (dec) 34 *K6, p2tog, p3; rep from * around—80 sts.
Rnd 35 *K6, p4; rep from * around.
Rnd 36 *6-st RC, p4; rep from * around.
Rnd (dec) 37 *K6, p2tog, p2; rep from * around—72 sts.
Rnd (dec) 38 *K5, k2tog, p2—64 sts.
Rnd (dec) 39 *K5, k2tog, p1—56 sts.
Rnd (dec) 40 *K5, k2tog—48 sts.
Rnd (dec) 41 *K4, k2tog—40 sts.
Rnd (dec) 42 *K3, k2tog—32 sts.
Rnd (dec) 43 *K2, k2tog—24 sts.
Rnd (dec) 44 *K1, k2tog—16 sts.
Rnd (dec) 45 [K2tog] 8 times—8 sts. Cut yarn leaving a 8"/20.5cm tail and thread through rem sts. Pull tog tightly and secure end.

FLOWER Topped

YOU'LL NEED:

YARN
1¾oz/50g or 80yd/70m of any
worsted weight wool blend yarn
in light blue (A), blue (B), and light
green (C)

NEEDLES
1 set (4) size 7 (4.5mm) double-
pointed needles (dpns)
or size to obtain gauge
Size 7 (4.5mm) circular needle,
16"/40cm long

ADDITIONAL MATERIALS
Size G/6 (4.5mm) crochet hook

KNITTED MEASUREMENTS
Sized for Medium (Large/X-Large)
Circumference 20 (22½)"/51 (57)cm
Length 8½"/21.5cm

GAUGE
19 sts and 25 rows/rnds to 4"/10cm over St
st using size 7 (4.5mm) needles.
Take time to check gauge.

CAP
With circular needle and A, cast on 96 (108)
sts. Join and working in rnds, k1 rnd, p1
rnd. Change to B.
Beg wave pat
Rnd 1 *K1, yo, k4, SK2P, k4, yo; rep from *
7 (8) times more.
Rnd 2 and all even rnds Purl.
Note Be sure to p the final yo from rnd 1 or
the st count will not remain the same.
Rnd 3 K2, *yo, k3, SK2P, k3, yo, k3; rep from
*, ending last rep k1 instead of k3. **Rnd 5** K3,
*yo, k2, SK2P, k2, yo, k5; rep from * ending
last rep k2 instead of k5. **Rnd 7** K4, *yo, k1,
SK2P, k1, yo, k7; rep from * ending last rep
k3 instead of k7. **Rnd 9** K5, *yo, SK2P, yo, k9;
rep from * ending last rep k4 instead of k9.
Rnd 10 Purl.
**Change to A and k1 rnd, p1 rnd (for
garter ridge). Change to C.
Beg wave pat
Rnd 1 Knit. **Rnd 2** P3, [k7, p5] 7 (8) times,

Eye[4]Media

k7, p2. **Rnd 3** K2, *p2, k5, p2, k3; rep from *
ending last rep k1, instead of k3. **Rnd 4** K3,
*p2, k3, p2, k5; rep from * ending last rep k2
instead of k5. **Rnd 5** K4, [p5, k7] 7 (8) times,
p5, k3. Change to A and k1 rnd, p1 rnd.
Change to B and work rnds 1–5 of wave
pat once, rnds 2–5 once. Rep from ** once
more. Change to A and k1 rnd, p1 rnd.
Shape crown
Change to C.
Rnd 1 and all odd rnds Knit. **Rnd 2** *K1,
k2tog, k11 (13), k2tog tbl; rep from *
around—84 (96) sts. **Rnd 4** *K1, k2tog, k9
(11), k2tog tbl; rep form * around—72 (84)
sts. **Rnd 6** *K1, k2tog, k7 (9), k2tog tbl; rep
from * around—60 (72) sts.
Rnd 8 *K1, k2tog, k5 (7) k2tog tbl; rep from
* around—48 (60) sts. Change to dpns to
accommodate the fewer sts.
Rnd 10 *K1, k2tog, k 3 (5), k2tog tbl; rep
from * around—36 (48) sts.
Rnd 12 *K1, k2tog, k1 (3), k2tog tbl; rep
from * around—24 (36) sts.
Size medium only
Rnd 14 K2tog, pass last st from previous
rnd over this st, k1, *SK2P, k1; rep from *,

rep—12 sts.
Rnd 16 [K3tog] 4 times—4 sts rem.
Size large/X-large only
Rnd 14 *K1, k2tog, k1, k2tog tbl; rep from *
around—24 sts. **Rnd 16** K2tog, pass last st
from previous rnd over this st, k1, *SK2P, k1;
rep from *, omitting the k1 on last rep —12
sts. **Rnd 17** [K3tog] 4 times—4 sts rem.
Both sizes
Cut yarn and pull through rem 4 sts and
draw up tightly to secure top.

FINISHING
Block lightly, pinning lower edge to
form points.
Flower
With crochet hook and A, ch 50.
Rnd 1 Sc in 2nd ch from hook and in each
ch to end. Fasten off. With B, work another
ch in same way. Fold A ch into 3 lps and
fasten to top of cap. Fold B ch into 3 lps
and fasten in an alternating flower style on
top of A lps.

BRAIDED Trim

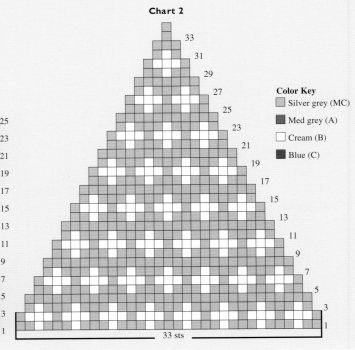

Eye4Media

YOU'LL NEED:

YARN
2 1¾oz/50g balls (each approx 203yd/186m) of Patons® *Kroy* (wool/nylon) in silver grey (MC). 1 ball each in med grey (A), cream (B), and blue (C)

NEEDLES
One pair size 2 (2.75mm) needles
or size to obtain gauge
One set (5) size 2 (2.75mm) double-pointed needles (dpns)

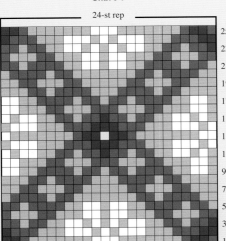

KNITTED MEASUREMENTS
Circumference 20"/51cm
Length (excluding earflaps) 8½"/21.5cm

GAUGE
30 sts and 39 rows to 4"/10cm over St st foll chart using size 2 (2.75mm) needle. *Take time to check gauge.*

NOTE
When changing colors foll chart, bring new yarn from underneath working yarn to avoid holes in work.

FIRST EARFLAP
Using straight needles, with MC, cast on 18 sts.

Row 1 (RS) Inc 1 st in first st, k to last 2 sts, inc 1 st in next st, k1.
Row 2 Purl.
Rep last 2 rows 4 times more—28 sts.
Next row Rep row 1—30 sts.
Work 3 rows even.
Rep last 4 rows once more—32 sts. Cut yarn and leave sts on spare needle.

SECOND EARFLAP
Work as for first earflap, only do not cut MC at end of working.

CAP

Joining row (RS)
With MC, cast on 17 sts, k32 sts from second earflap, turn. Cast on 52 sts, turn.
Next row Cont with MC, k32 sts of first earflap, turn. Cast on 17 sts—150 sts. Turn and working in rnds from this point on 4 dpn, join sts and pm to mark beg of rnd. Divide sts so there are 37 sts on 2 needles and 38 sts on 2 needles. With MC, k6 rnds
**Next rnd *With B, k1, with MC, k1, rep from * around.
Next (braided) rnd Working with both strands of yarn in front of work across the entire rnd, work as foll: *Bringing the next color to purl over the last st worked (this around), with B, p1, with MC, p1; rep from * around.
Next (braided) rnd Working with both strands of yarn in front of work across the entire rnd, *bringing the next color to purl under the last st (this untwists the yarn as you purl around), with B, p1, with MC, p1; rep from * around **.
+Rep between **'s once, only substitute MC for B and A for MC. Rep between **'s once using colors as described +. With A, k6 rnds.
Rep between +'s once.
Next rnd With MC, *k7, inc 1 st in the next st; rep from * 17 times more—168 sts.

Beg chart 1
Rnd 1 Working rnd 1 of chart 1, work 24-st rep 7 times around. Cont to foll chart 1 through rnd 25.
Next rnd With MC, *k12, k2tog; rep from * 11 times more—156 sts.
Next rnd *With MC, k1, with A, k1; rep from * around.
Next (braided) rnd Working with both strands of yarn in front of work across entire rnd, work as foll: * bringing the next color to purl over the last st worked (this will twist the yarn as you purl

Chart 1
24-st rep

25
23
21
19
17
15
13
11
9
7
5
3
1

Chart 2
33
31
29
27
25
23
21
19
17
15
13
11
9
7
5
3
1

33 sts

Color Key
- Silver grey (MC)
- Med grey (A)
- Cream (B)
- Blue (C)

Bobb Connors

around), with MC, p1, with A, p1; rep from *
around.
Next rnd With MC, knit.
Shape top
Beg chart 2
Rnd 1 *With MC, k1, SKP, work rnd 1 of chart
2 across next 33 sts, with MC, k2tog, k1; rep
from * 3 times more.
Rnd 2 *With MC, k2, work rnd 2 of chart 2
across next 33 sts, with MC, k2; rep from * 3
times more.
Rnd 3 *With MC, k1, SKP, work rnd 3 of chart
2 across next 31 sts, with MC, k2tog, k1; rep
from * 3 times more.
Rnd 4 *With MC, k2, work rnd 4 of chart 2
across next 31 sts, with MC, k2; rep from *
3 times more. Cont to work chart 2 in this
way, dec 8 sts in MC every alternate rnd as
established until chart 2 is completed and
20 sts rem. Cut yarn leaving end for sewing
top. Pull through rem 20 sts on needles and
draw up tightly to secure. Fasten off.

FINISHING
Block flat to measurements.
Lower edge trim
Beg at the center back of cap, with RS facing,
A and 4 dpn, pick up and k sts as foll: 17 sts
from lower back cast-on edge, 13 sts along
shaped edge of first earflap, 18 sts along
cast-on edge of earflap, 13 sts along other
shaped edge of earflap, 52 sts from first
cast-on edge, 13 sts along shaped edge of
second earflap,
18 sts along cast-on edge of earflap, 13 sts
along other shaped edge of earflap, 17 sts
from lower back cast-on edge—174 sts.
Join
and work in rnds. Pm to mark beg of rnd.
Next rnd *With A, k1, with B, k1; rep from *
around.
Next (braided) rnd Working with both
strands of yarn in front of work across the
entire rnd, work as foll: *bringing the next
color to purl over the last st worked (this
will twist the yarn as you purl around), with
A, p1, with B, p1; rep from * around. With A,
k8 rnds. Bind off. Fold edging along braided
rnd to WS and sew in place.
Braid
Cut 26 strands each of colors MC, A and B
at 14"/36cm long. Make a braid as shown,
wrapping MC around ends. Attach to top
of cap.

YOU'LL NEED:
YARN 🟢6
3½oz/100g or 70yd/60m of any
super-bulky wool blend yarn

NEEDLES
One each sizes 10½ and 11 (6.5 and
8mm) circular needle, 16"/40cm long
or size to obtain gauge
One set (5) size 11 (8mm) double-
pointed needles (dpns)

ADDITIONAL MATERIALS
Stitch markers

KNITTED MEASUREMENTS
Circumference 18⅝"/47.2cm
Length 9"/22.9cm

GAUGE
12 sts and 13 rnds to 4"/10cm over St
st, using larger needles.
Take time to check gauge.

NOTES
1 Piece is shown in reverse St st. For
ease in working, work in St st and
turn inside out at completion.
2 Change to dpns when there are
too few sts to fit comfortably on the
circular needle.

STITCH GLOSSARY
K1, P1 Twisted Rib
Rnd 1 *K1 tbl, p1; rep from * around.
Rep rnd 1 for k1, p1 twisted rib.

CAP
With smaller needle, cast on 56 sts.
Join, taking care not to twist sts on
needle. Mark end of rnd and sl marker
every rnd. Work in k1, p1 rib twisted
rib for 4 rnds. Turn piece to WS.
Change to larger needle and k 2 rnds.
Beg slant pat
Rnd 1 *SKP, k4, yo, k2; rep from *
around. Rep this rnd 15 times more.
Next (dec) rnd *SKP, k6; rep from *
around. **Next (dec) rnd** *SKP, k5; rep
from * around. **Next (dec) rnd** *SKP,
k4; rep from * around.
Change to dpns and cont to dec in
this way until 14 sts rem.
Next (dec) rnd SKP around—7 sts.
Place rem sts on 2 dpn and work
I-cord as foll: *slide sts to beg of
needle without turning, k7; rep from *
4 times more. Pull yarn through rem 7
sts. Draw up tightly and fasten off.

FINISHING
Block piece. Turn piece so that reverse
St st side is showing. Pull top of
I-cord into center to form button (see
photo).

NEWSBOY Cap

YOU'LL NEED:

YARN
4oz/113g or 140yd/130m of any bulky
weight self-striping wool yarn

NEEDLES
One set (5) size 10½ (6.5mm)
double-pointed needles (dpns)
or size to obtain gauge

ADDITIONAL MATERIALS
Stitch markers

KNITTED MEASUREMENTS
Circumference 18¼"/46.5cm
Length 8¾"/22cm

GAUGE
14 sts and 24 rows to 4"/10cm over garter rib using size 10½ (6.5mm) needles.
Take time to check gauge.

STITCH GLOSSARY
Garter Rib
Rnd 1 *K2, p2; rep from * around.
Rnd 2 Knit.

BEANIE
Using size 10½ (6.5mm) dpns, cast on 64
sts. Join, being careful not to twist sts,
place marker for beg of rnd. Work in gar-
ter rib until piece measures 8"/20.5cm
from beg, end with a rnd 1.
Shape crown
Rnd 1 (dec) *K2tog; rep from *
around—32 sts.
Rnd 2 K 1 rnd.
Rep rnds 1 and 2 once more—16 sts,
Next rnd K2tog around—8 sts.
Cut yarn, leaving 12"/30.5cm tail. Thread
yarn through rem sts. Fasten off.